Keep Your Ass in the Saddle

How a Farm, a Fire, and Failure Led Me to Freedom

ANNIE M. FONTE

outskirts
press

Dedication
To you, the reader ...
May you have the courage to let go
of the things not meant for you,
and the wisdom to know that you are
the only superhero you will ever need.

Caleb -
May you find some inspiration
words of wisdom : inspiration
among these pages.
All my best,
Annie
+ 2024!

ACKNOWLEDGMENTS

Being first can be exhilarating, or it can be bumpy, vague, and ever-changing depending on the role you are playing.

Many people read some form of the words on these pages long before they were squeezed between a shiny cover and became a book. Thank you to my tribe of firsts—the pre-book readers who patiently waded through early and undone versions and generously gave me feedback, encouragement, inspiration, and support. A few even told me that I wasn't done writing when I was sure that I was.

Then there were the listeners. Steve and Helen DiZio were stuck in a vehicle with me for hours as we traveled through Death Valley on our way to a Cowboy Poetry event. I read. They listened. I want to think that they were so riveted by the story that we almost ran out of gas. It turns out that wasn't the case. We almost ran out of gas the following year in the same spot going to the same place. Thanks, guys.

My pal, Andrea Leonard, listened to me read my story to her on many occasions long before the book was a wrap. Quite a bit of wine was involved. It helped both of us. Cheers, my friend.

My mom has also listened from the beginning. Every Monday evening I would read to her over the phone. Me in California, she in Colorado in the small town where this whole tale started. Thank you for lending an ear to what much of had to be hard to hear.

As far as brothers go, I have the best. Thank you, Dan, for having my back my entire life. You have shown me how to live life with grace and perseverance and realness. We have been through a lot together, and you have always made the ride smoother. You make me want to be a better person.

I would be remiss if I didn't express my gratitude to my dog, Porkchop. I was blessed with his daily companionship for 11 years. He never left my side as he generously provided the loyalty and steadfast comfort I needed to rebuild a house, navigate a lawsuit, and traverse the tumultuous waters of heartbreak. Thank you for the countless memories and the love that you gave so freely. You taught me so much about life. Not a day goes by that I don't think about you and smile.

And finally, there's you, God. Thank you for sitting on my bed and talking to me during the doubtful days of my childhood. And, as an adult you have listened to me ramble on; I have told you my plans, and I have been pissed off at You, and I have questioned You and sometimes wondered how disappointment and anguish can be Your gifts to me. But I have come to know that my greatest blessings have come from things that don't make sense to me and that You are behind it all. Thank you for your patience. You are the Man.

TABLE OF CONTENTS

INTRODUCTION

Who decides to write a book and why? There are people out there who love to write. They have a way with words, and they provide intrigue, entertainment, information, and adventure to readers. And—with some luck—they make a difference with their words. Why did I decide to write a book?

Well, it isn't because I love to write—although I do a fair amount of it. It isn't something I do because I have an overwhelming passion for the craft or feel like I must write my every thought down as a memento to myself or others. I wrote this book because I have a story to tell.

It is a story of grit, gratitude, badassery, and determination. I wrote this book because I believe, in these pages, you will read about courage, hope, and passion, with a touch of humor along the way. I wrote this book because I want you to know that anything is possible if you believe it is.

I want you to know that the only limitations in your life are the ones you give yourself, that the only foundation on which to build a life you love is through authenticity. Life is only as complicated as you decide to make it. The process of writing this book has taken me completely out of my comfort zone, but I believe that's where the magic lies.

I wrote this simply so that, in hearing my story, it will help you acknowledge, honor, and appreciate your own life story. I want to help you experience the beauty of being alive and help you to create a life that you love and deserve. A well-known poet named Rilke once said, "Being here is so much." It's so true.

The traditional structures of family, parenting, community, and communication have become increasingly unsure. We lose sight of the reliable presence and repetitions of the stars, sun, moon, and seasons. Our lives become predictable, and our behaviors become routine and mindless; we lose ourselves in the daily mechanical functioning of our lives.

We take the same route to the office each day, park in the same parking spot; we eat our meals at the same time, and often eat the same thing. We interact with friends and colleagues with little presence or creativity, rarely stepping out of our comfort zone.

We begin to develop patterns of thinking, rendering us incapable of feeling or thinking with any authenticity or refinement. We have handed much of our daily living over to smartphones, social media, and mindless consumption. It is only when something throws a wrench into our drone-like existence that we wake up to the beauty of knowing that "being here is so much."

It is the diagnosis of a terminal illness, the unexpected death of a loved one, the loss of a job, or some other sudden disruption of our comfort and familiarity that awakens us to the gifts of the world. And so, I encourage you to be still long enough to realize where you are, and who you are.

Don't wait for heartbreak or misfortune to rattle you to your core before you become fully alive. Be badass. Courageously walk into—and through—uncertainty, discomfort, and fear, because on the other side is where you will find frontiers of possibility. That is when, possibly for the first time, you will fully understand and embrace that "being here is so much."

I believe that if I am going to write about farming and hardship and growing up gritty and straying so far from my authenticity that I didn't recognize myself, I shouldn't do it from the cheap seats. My words come from a place deep inside of me that has captured moments, days, and seasons of my life.

Over the years I have tucked away the lessons that I have learned, and I can no longer ignore the gentle, yet persistent nudge that wants me to share them with you. As you read these pages, I hope that you will laugh a little, you might shed a tear or two, but this is no sob story. There is no whining—no need for it. This story isn't about me. It is for you.

Throughout these pages, you will see opportunities to pause and reflect. The situations and events that you have encountered in your life will not be the same as mine. However, I want you to know that I stand shoulder-to-shoulder with you as you stop to consider the impact that people, places, and things have had on your life.

I don't consider this to be a self-help or personal development book. Instead, I want it to serve as encouragement and inspiration to you. I want you to fall in love with who you are, realize your desires, and live your life full-out. Because guess what? **If I can do it, so can you.**

WHY PAUSE, AND WHY IS IT IMPORTANT?

It is the pause between the action that makes for a great life. Robert Fripp, the legendary guitarist, explains, "The music is between the notes, not in the notes." A pause isn't a time of "nothing"; it is a time of possibility. It gives you a chance to catch up to yourself.

The break allows you to heal from wounds that you have sustained on your journey. It means that you care enough about yourself that you are willing to stop and linger in those moments of prospect. Tara Brach, the author of Radical Acceptance, writes this in her book: "Through the sacred art of pausing, we develop the capacity to stop hiding, to stop running away from our own experience. We begin to trust in our natural intelligence, in our naturally wise heart, in our capacity to open to what arises."

I found this to be true in my journey. It was the quiet moments that gave me the courage and the freedom to accept where I was and to trust where I was heading. I summon you to do the same for yourself. Take the time to take the time. Stop long enough to be with yourself. Be still. The stillness is the background that allows future movement to be well informed, inspired, and stunningly valuable.

What Is Reflection?

Self-reflection is giving careful thought to your behavior and beliefs. It is an opportunity to exercise introspection and to learn more about yourself. When I reflect on times in my childhood, I can see the innocence of a young girl, and yet, I recognize the old-soul wisdom that existed long before I took full embrace of it.

Now, at the end of the day, when I spend a few minutes thinking about the hours behind me and what I learned, I discover a closer connection to myself. I appraise the delights of the day and isolate the leeway for growth and grace. Whatever your situation or wherever you are in your life, give yourself the gift of reflection.

By taking the time to pause and look within, you will discern that you have many of the answers to your questions. This time of contemplation gives you the chance to confront your thoughts and limiting beliefs. Remember, the things that you tell yourself are only true if you imagine that they are.

Self-reflection ushers you to self-awareness, where you can gain clarity about your emotions and desires. Here is where our trustworthy, yet often-ignored pal, intuition, is given a seat at the table. I genuinely believe that each of us has an invaluable but underutilized resource that we carry around with us 24/7, and that is our "gut."

It is our inner knowing. Listen to it, use it, trust it. And finally, the grand prize of self-reflection is self-acceptance. It isn't until we meet ourselves where we are that we can take ourselves where we want to go.

FOREWORD

I have known Annie for more than two decades, her deep soul authenticity in this book has made me feel privileged to know her and call her a dear eternal friend and that is a treasure which is hard to come by.

This book is a page-turner! I usually feel triumphant after I read the final page of a book. And even so, I went back after a couple of days and reread the last few chapters, this time with my journal and time to write and reflect. I promise, *Keep Your Ass In The Saddle* is required reading!

I don't see this as a self-help book and here's why. I see this as an opportunity to have a safe, honest conversation with yourself while in the presence of someone who has taken the time to courageously have it with herself first. I have a bullshit detector and no tolerance for the 'messenger' who is a preacher in public and a liar after the applause.

Excavating the past from childhood is not something I'm usually a fan of because life is a fast forward moving bulldozer these days and often digging through a closet of skeletons can get you stuck in self-pity and victimhood. But Annie has proved the opposite. As a young child, she was driving combines and tractors and was expected to contribute to the farming as well as help tend to cattle in the dead of winter all while navigating the heavy-handed parenting of her dad. Twelve hour days in the fields operating massive pieces of equipment with a baloney sandwich and a beer for nourishment were the norm. But in spite of and because of it, Annie has heroically translated her youth and adolescence into the powerful, kind and capable woman she is and has earned the right to teach us how to keep our asses in the saddles of our lives. And that's a tall order!

In Annie's chapter about her relationship with Gene, it activated for me the situations I found myself in where I also had feelings of 'self-doubt, dismay, mistrust, and unease.' To acknowledge that one has allowed an intimate partner to devalue and demean you is the hard first step you must take to climb out of the depths of despair and rekindle the love for yourself that's necessary for a bright future. It takes courage but also skilled guidance, which Annie brilliantly assists in traversing those minefields back to who you truly are.

It's hard to identify a narcissist at the beginning of a relationship because they have a stellar act. Charming and confident, they're usually successful and admired. And they seem to adore you, but there are little warning signs that you are (nearly) blind to because they are Academy Award-winning actors. This chapter caused me to grab my journal again and reflect on any lingering beliefs I had that lurked in the history of my life.

The list at the end of Chapter 29 is the best roadmap to unraveling and reconstructing the absolute most crucial thing in anyone's life. It's a rare opportunity to see what makes Annie tick and why her life is so remarkable and unique today. I know it's because she lives by her pledges and promises consistently and reverently.

'You are worth fighting for.'

Becky Robbins, author, philanthropist, artist
www.beckyrobbins.com

Chapter One

COMING HOME

"To me she was those final steps, and the turn around the bend, the house with a light on and a fire lit and a faint laugh on warm wind—she was always my coming home."

— Atticus

I SAT THERE on that blustery Colorado day, staring out onto a wheat field that seemed to stretch all the way to the end of the earth as it pushed against a cashmere grey sky. My heart pounded, recognizing how appropriate the setting was. Here I was, back to where I grew up. My roots—farmland as far as you could see.

I stood up and took a single red carnation from my brother as several mourners had done before me. I walked to the edge and looked down. I gazed into a perfectly groomed, six-foot-deep grave, and thought to myself, *Fuck. That sucks.* The view was cold, lonely, and dark. In that moment, it occurred to me that to get to heaven from that hole in the ground was no easy journey, especially if you had to go through hell to get there.

I leaned over the casket and firmly placed my flower among those already resting there. While others were saying their sad good-byes, some struggling to hold back tears, I felt relief. He was gone now, and a sense of freedom came over me. It was a big day for me. Now that he was gone, I could break out of the lifelong embrace of that horrible monster who occupied valuable space in my mind.

It was my Independence Day. It was the day we buried him. His name was George. He was my dad. And, his favorite flower was a red carnation. This day also marked the beginning of my journey back to myself.

The way I see it, we have two parts of ourselves. One is the physical, skin-and-bones being who walks around the planet, cries and laughs, loves and aches, and overthinks just about everything.

The other is the observer. The one who is patiently watching us go through the motions of being human. My observer is my North Star. My compass, my loyal and trustworthy friend, my true essence. She is me, free of the human condition. We started out as one, and we stuck together for a very long time. And then, I left her.

I allowed the noise of the world, and fear, and ego, and all the other bullshit that comes along with uncertainty and lack of clarity to push her away. I unintentionally abandoned her. But she stuck with me through all of my insecurities, bad decisions, and uninspired actions.

She unwaveringly watched as I stumbled around, ignoring her wisdom, yet she kept the door open for me to come back to her. She steadfastly knew that someday I would once again come home to my authentic self. I have come to call this "*keeping my ass in the saddle.*"

George's death sparked the start of my voyage back to saving myself and recapturing my genuineness. The trek was scary—gut-wrenching at times—ambiguous, lonely, and rife with unexpected landmines. It was also fun, funny, stunning, exciting, and eye-opening. Ultimately, it led me to a life of absolute freedom and the courage to be myself.

My father's death played a notable role as the catalyst to commencing my essential life transformation. There were over four decades of my existence that led up to it. Let's start at the beginning, shall we?

Chapter Two

IN THE BEGINNING

"Childhood is the one story that stands by itself in every soul."
— Ivan Doig

JULY 25TH, 8:47 am. It was a Monday morning. The doctor smacked me on the ass and I took my first breath, letting out a robust cry, announcing my arrival into the world. I wasn't due for a few more weeks, but my mom had me via cesarean section, so they "took me early."

My mom told me she was sick from the moment of my conception until the moment I was born. That should have told her something about what kind of kid I would be. It was her dream and vision that her little girl would love to wear frilly dresses, want to play the piano, dance around sweetly with bows in her hair, and grow up to be a nurse, just like her. Guess what? None of that happened.

I preferred blue jeans, t-shirts, and cowboy boots. Still do. I wanted to play sports, not the piano. Girly-girls pissed me off, and I couldn't fathom being a nurse. Don't get me wrong—I think nurses are some of God's angels on earth, and my mom was one of the best. I just wasn't cut out for that particular job.

I was born a healthy seven pounds and fourteen ounces, with almond-shaped eyes and a yellow discoloration in my skin, medically known as jaundice. The first time George saw me, he told my mom it was "a nice baby she had," as if there was no way he had anything to do with such a homely and tarnished creature.

I was my mom's firstborn child and George's second. Before marrying my mom, George was married to a woman named Dora. She was the love of his life. They had a son whom they called Michael. Dora died while delivering their baby boy, leaving George with a brand-new child and a grieving heart. I cannot imagine the overwhelming anguish such a tragic and unexpected event must have brought to him.

Eight months after Dora's death, my parents said their "I dos," and nine months later, I joined them and Mike, who I have only known as my older brother my entire life; Mike, having a different biological mother, was never mentioned during our childhood.

Building our family came with its fair share of sorrow. Eighteen months after I was born, my mom had my baby brother, Andy.

She carried him full-term and experienced a conventional pregnancy. However, thirty-six hours after his birth, he died of a congenital heart defect. This was another unforeseen episode of heartbreak, permeating what is customarily a time of incredible joy. The loss of Andy was uniquely confronting for two reasons: 1) my parents desperately wanted another boy, and 2) the doctors strongly urged my mom not to have any more children.

Undeterred, George and my mom transcended heartbreak and potential hazard and, seventeen months later, my younger brother, Dan, blessed our family. I didn't experience the emotion of loss when Andy died because I was too young. My mom showed me pictures of him, and all I can remember is that he was a gorgeous little guy with thick black hair.

As I've thought about Andy over the years, I bet he would have been a fantastic brother. But I also believe God takes his angels when he needs them. If Andy would have lived, then Dan wouldn't have been born. So the way I look at it is, God got one hell of an angel, and I got one hell of a brother.

I'm not sure how far back most people can remember, I guess it's probably different for everyone, but I do remember when my little brother was a baby. His given name is Daniel, but everyone calls him Dan. He was cute and fat, with reddish-blond, curly hair, light skin, and blue eyes.

When we got a bit older, I questioned who his parents were, because—as far as I was concerned—we didn't look anything alike. I had dark hair, dark skin, arrow-straight hair, green eyes, and was as skinny as a rail. There was no way the same people could have created such mismatched siblings. It turned out we did have the same parents, but it wouldn't have mattered to me, because I loved that fat, happy, blue-eyed boy so much.

Dan was joyful all the time, especially when he was eating. I have vivid memories of him sitting in his high chair for hours, jolly as could be, eating Oreo cookies. He celebrated getting just as much cookie all over his body as he did in his mouth.

My mom would bathe him in the kitchen sink and he loved it. I would pull up a chair and somehow manage to shimmy myself in the middle so I could help. Baby Dan would giggle the whole time, his chubby legs and potbelly utterly delighted by the entire experience of splashing around in the warm, soothing water.

Not only was I his big sister, I was also his protector, teacher, interpreter, playmate, and constant sidekick. Dan had an imaginary friend from the time he was about two years old. This "friend" went everywhere with him. We set a place at the table for him and made room for him in the truck, bathtub, couch, and bed.

Dan and his friend would have full-on conversations with each other, at least to the extent of a two-year-old. This fantasy relationship went on for many months. Then, one day—he was gone. It was as simple as that: just plain gone with no explanation. We all got in the pickup one day, and I did what I had grown accustomed to doing—I made room for the "friend." Dan merely shook his head from side to side, and bluntly said: "He's gone." That was it. We never talked about it again.

Not too long after the "friend" went away, Mike, Dan, and I got all bundled up to go outside to play in the snow on one cold Colorado winter's day. Dan looked like the Michelin Man, stuffed into his snow-suit with his little rubber boots housing his wobbly feet. We ended up at the stock tanks—these large, round water reservoirs located about fifty feet from the house from which our cattle would drink.

They would often get a layer of ice when temperatures would dip below thirty-two degrees. In the summer, they doubled as our swim-ming pool. We could spend hours in those tanks, splashing around in moss-filled water, having the time of our lives. We would take oc-casional breaks to lie on the sun-warmed sidewalks to dry off, before heading back in to share the "pool" with an occasional cow who came by for a drink of water.

However, on this particular winter's day, we wanted to test the thickness of the ice to see if we could walk on it, which was one of the many great ideas we came up with being raised on a farm with so many opportunities to create havoc. Thus, there the three of us stood. Dan hobbled first, and the next thing I knew, he had fallen into the tank, slipping under the ice and into the freezing water below.

I was scared to death. But, as if I had done it a thousand times before, I reached in and grabbed him by his snowsuit, yanking him out from under the ice and onto the ground. His big blue eyes looked at me with great surprise, but not one tear in them. My first thought was how bad we were going to get our asses tanned from George's belt. That was always the punishment for our "crimes."

The extent or intent of our so-called lousy behavior had no bear-ing on the level of penalty we received. A two-inch-wide belt, folded in half, in the grip of our angry—and often forceful—dad was the condemnation of choice. We usually had a little time to prepare for our encounters with "the belt," so the three of us would convene to help each other pad up for the event.

We would put layers of clothes on and stuff t-shirts in the back of our pants to soften the blow of our ass-beating. Then, we would give each other a pep talk to remind one another to be brave. And, for God's sake, don't cry because one of George's favorite things to say while he was pummeling us, was, "You want to cry?! I'll give you something to cry about!"

The padding eased some of the stings as the belt met our tender flesh. Most of the time during these lashings, we managed to hold back the tears—even me. It was always a relief when these encounters ended, but the proof lingered for several days until the welts on our asses and the backs of our legs lost their luster. In my mind, though, the frequency of "getting the belt" was not congruent with our behavior.

All in all, I thought we were pretty good kids. As a youngster, I didn't understand why this guy was so angry all the time. I thought dads were supposed to love and care for their children, keep them out of harm's way, and provide them with the support they needed to thrive.

I wanted to trust that I was safe around him. Regrettably, I learned at a very young age that the only person who was going to take care of me, was me. So, while slowly concluding George's behavior was not okay (and later realizing it was textbook narcissism), I quietly and most certainly became a badass.

PAUSE AND REFLECT: BECOMING A BADASS

Not long ago, someone asked me how I got to be a badass. It's a good question, and before I answer it, let me explain to you what I consider badass:

- You are badass if you courageously walk into and through uncertainty, discomfort, and fear, trusting that on the other side you will find yourself in one piece.

- A badass sculpts their unique path. They have a distinctive style. They are not concerned with fitting in, but instead, resolute in figuring it out, whatever it is.

I think I was born a badass, or at least with a propensity toward badassery. Some things you just are, there is no fighting it. As a very young girl, I remember being afraid of George. He seemed angry a lot. He often took his ire out on my brothers and me in the form of yelling at us or employing his belt to discipline us for what he perceived as bad behavior.

Our mom never questioned his despotic approach to child rearing, as I think she was as wary of him as I was. And so, it began. When I was quite young, I tuned in to the fact that these people I thought would keep me safe and watch over me and guide me, were not up for the job.

They had other things on their mind, like nursing and farming, and self-preservation—all the while keeping a roof over our head and some food in our bellies. I'm not so sure how brave I was, but I marched straight into uncertainty, discomfort, and fear most days of my childhood with no measure of trust I would come out the other side at all, let alone in one piece.

I unwittingly armored up and did my best to stay off the radar of George's outbursts. I spent a lot of time by myself, committed to getting through my doubt one day at a time—a badass in the making each step of the way.

Badassery has served me well over the years. For me, it is a way of being that reminds me to be resolute in taking responsibility for my thoughts and actions. It is not about being mean or unapproachable or having a chip on my shoulder. Rather, it is acting in a way that's aligned with my authenticity.

Please don't allow people or situations that you encounter in your life to harden you. You have a choice in the matter. Be a badass instead. Be accountable, be brave, and figure it out.

Becoming a Farmer

When all the other girls wanted to be princesses, I wanted to be a farmer. My brothers and I were all very young when we started driving tractors, pickups, combines, swathers, and anything else that had an engine and was needed to farm. At the ripe old age of four, George would put me behind the wheel of our pickup truck and point to a fence post in the distance he wanted me to steer toward while he threw hay out of the back of the truck to feed the cattle.

I was about thirty-seven inches tall at the time, so I would kneel up on the seat to see over the steering wheel and focus with laser-beam intent on my target. The pickup would go on its own, eliminating the need to manage the gas pedal. We all had years of observation time under our belts before we were planted in a John Deere tractor seat to pilot our own rigs.

Our mom worked every day at the hospital, so in the summer, when we weren't in school, George was our babysitter. We spent a lot of time with him, going everywhere together. We would all climb aboard a John Deere tractor, Mike and I each on a fender, and Dan, strapped to the back of the seat and the power take-off bar. Our dog, Duke, would loyally follow along behind.

We would ride for hours, round after round, acre after acre, field after field, day after day until we finished one of the several stages of the farming season. We all sat out in the open air with the only slice of protection from the sun being a canvas shade mounted on brackets on top of the fenders.

It was hot, dusty, and noisy. In the early afternoons, George would make a little spot at the end of the field where the three of us would take a nap with Duke. An hour or so later, refreshed from our short slumber, we would catch up to George and, once again, occupy our post on the green, rumbling machine.

I didn't mind the heat. I grew to love the smell of freshly churned earth and, to this day, the sound of a diesel engine brings a smile to my face and makes my heart race with pride—something only a farm girl can appreciate. All those hours I sat on that fender gave me time to study the craft of driving a massive machine that was pulling a substantial piece of equipment, doing this thing called "farming."

I watched the gauges, watched how George managed the hydraulics that raised and lowered the apparatus in and out of the ground; I carefully observed the finesse it took to use the turning brakes to make the perfect direction-change at the end of the field. I asked tons of questions because I wanted to be at the helm of that tractor one day.

The first of us to occupy the tractor seat to assist George was my oldest brother, Mike. He didn't like the idea at all, and with good reason. George was tough. He expected a lot, he had a bad temper, and he focused on what was wrong with any situation far more than what was right.

What he lacked in inspiration, he made up for in heavy-handed discipline and loudness, pointing out how stupid we all were, regardless of our best intentions. I'll never forget the day I was in the field with George, me on one tractor, he on the other. My job was to work the terraces. (Terraces are man-made earthen structures designed to eliminate water runoff and erosion on farmland. They are groomed differently than the rest of a field to make sure that the integrity of the land doesn't deteriorate over time.)

A mere fifty yards separated us, and I saw him waving his hands in the air at me. I waved back, thinking he was giving me an "atta girl" signal. Next thing I knew, he stopped his rig, jumped off, and came storming toward me with big, purposeful, angry strides. When he got to my tractor, he yelled, "Shut that goddamn thing down!" I immediately throttled down the engine to an idle and brought my rig to a standstill.

The next thing I remember, I was being dragged off my tractor to the ground, and he was spinning me in circles—kicking my ass, literally. George was full-on pissed off, and I had no idea why. When he was finished planting his boot in my ass, he proceeded to tell me I was doing the exact opposite of what he had told me to do. My self-pride and confidence were shattered—I thought I was doing exactly what he told me to do (and, in my adolescent brain, doing it better than anyone else who had ever lived).

I climbed back up on that tractor, sat my tiny ass in that seat, got my rig sorted out, and—with tears streaming down my dirty face—I swore I would never make another mistake. Ever. My heart was broken and, as far as I was concerned, it was one of the few things in the universe that baling wire or duct tape couldn't patch back together.

Pause and Reflect: Loving Yourself

I think about how imperative it is to bolster yourself up during difficult times. I acknowledge the importance of clear communication, especially when teaching young kids, and that we cannot blame others for how our life looks and feels. We must stop holding on to toxins from our past. There are two energies of transformation: one is gratitude, and the other is forgiveness.

Love yourself enough to free yourself from the past. It is likely that you have experienced a situation in your past similar to what I did in my youth. Don't let whatever it was harden you. Resisting forgiveness will keep you stuck. If you have concocted a story about it that does not serve you, change the story.

I invite you to stop opening up doors from the past, and in doing so, you make space that can be filled up with whatever will allow you to evolve to your highest potential. Embody all that you want to be and choose to see yourself as worthy.

Pause and Reflect: Parenting

I am not a parent. I made this choice many years ago. I know now that I would have been an amazing mom. I don't say this to brag; it is simply a fact. I adore children. I have and will continue to do a lot for those precious souls that I know that I can help and inspire in some way.

Several years ago, I figured out why I chose a life without kids. There are two reasons; whether reasonable or not, here they are:

1) I was given a tremendous amount of responsibility at such a young age. You will read about it in the pages that follow. So, when I got to the time in my life when a child or two could have been brought into the fold, I decided that I did not want to take on more duty. The way I see it, parenting is the most crucial vocation there is, and with that comes heaps of responsibility.

2) George struggled as a parent, and if there was the slightest possibility that this trait could be passed along to me, I wasn't willing to risk it. I was not game to treat another human, especially an innocent child, the same way that he treated my brothers and me.

I am well aware that I would be completely out of my lane to think that I could give parenting advice. However, I once was a kid with parents. I know the impact that their behavior had on me, and so these are the questions I would ask people who are considering being or who are already moms and dads:

- What will be/are your values as a parent?
- Why do you want to be/are you a parent?
- Do you and your partner agree on a parenting style?
- How will you discipline your children?
- What values will you instill in your children?
- Are you willing to be truly present with your children?
- How will you communicate with your children?
- How will the world be a better place because you will be/are a parent?

In my case, I believe that my mom and dad did the best they could with the resources they had as parents. Parenting doesn't require one to pass a test or get a license. Babies don't come with a user's manual.

Most people are simply winging it when it comes to raising a child or children. Some people are naturals, while others struggle. George was one of the strugglers.

My mom had a career that she loved, and her income was a necessity for our family. Honestly, I think that they were doing their best to survive—as humans, as a couple, and as parents. They were both hard workers and if nothing else, they taught my brothers and me a strong work ethic which has served all of us well in our lives.

Chapter Three

YOU DON'T KNOW WHAT
YOU DON'T KNOW

"When nothing is sure, everything is possible."
— Margaret Drabble

IT WAS OUT of pure necessity that the three of us became farmhands. The days were long, and the pay was a bologna sandwich for lunch, chased down by a Coors Light. Yep, you read that right. We were young, determined, and hardworking, driving big pieces of equipment for hours on end, all while drinking a beer in the middle of the day.

As time went on, Mike was happy to pass the farming baton on to Dan and me, which was cool with us. Dan was born to farm; he was a natural. I loved Dan, and I loved being in the field with him. I especially liked the freedom of being out there all by ourselves.

Even though we were both under the age of ten, we knew what we were doing. At this point, George was spending his time going into town to play cards in the pool hall, while Dan and I groomed the land.

It was better with him not there.

If we broke down, we knew how to fix things, and together, Dan and I moved through vast acres of land with the effortlessness of the most beautifully choreographed dance you can imagine.

I was proud to sit on my tractor all day, tilling the ground in preparation for planting season. My tractor served as my sanctuary. It provided me the sense of peace and solace that I craved. Solitude was a much-desired and trustworthy companion I needed from a very young age. Those hours I spent sitting on a tractor nourished my innate need to devote unusual amounts of time to being alone.

I sang a lot. I sang loudly, as my competition was the big, husky voice of a diesel engine. Calamity Jane once said, "I figure, if a girl wants to be a legend, she should just go ahead and be one." So, I did. I was confident that I was one of the best singers on the planet as I rumbled along for hours singing some songs that I knew and making up lyrics for others that never amounted to much other than a product of my imagination.

When I wasn't singing, I was cloud-gazing. The Colorado skies are home to some of the most beautiful floating masses of condensed water vapor there are. As I crawled across the land in a swirl of dust, I would identify clouds in the crisp blue sky that looked like elephants and dogs and trees and monsters.

As the day wore on, they would change shape, and eventually give way to dusk. That was my favorite time of day—the quiet moments before sunset. My tractor ran better, I would get my second wind, and I would watch my dreams dance in the dust beams of a neon sky. How lucky I was to have all that alone time. Time to think, visualize, and create, limited only by my ingenuity.

It was during these days I would envision myself doing big things in the world. I saw myself carrying a briefcase and traveling in airplanes all over the place. I had no idea what existed outside the confines of the farm life I was born into, but I imagined a vast, big world with all kinds of possibilities.

Pause and Reflect: The Value of Visualization

I realized from the time I was quite young that I had good intuition. When I thought about things, the visions in my mind were as if a full-color movie was playing. This was a superpower as far as I was concerned because I had many hours during the day to focus on "what ifs."

I am especially thankful for the lack of distraction. My tractor didn't have a cab on it, which meant there was no radio. Cell phones weren't a thing yet and, even if they were, I am pretty sure I would not have had one. At the time, I didn't recognize my thoughts as visualizations, but in many ways, it saved me. It gave me hope.

It allowed me to imagine things that I wasn't even sure existed. To this day, I use visualization as a potent and trusted method for achieving what I desire in life. I encourage you to adopt a healthy visualization practice.

Here is a method that I use. I clearly define what I desire:

- What do I want to create in my life?
- How will this serve others?
- How will this serve me?
- What will it look like?
- How will it make me feel?
- Write a letter to myself titled "A Year from Now" that clearly defines all of the above and open it a year later.

Envision the version of myself who already has what I desire:

- How do I feel?
- What are my thoughts?
- What do I read?
- Who do I surround myself with?
- What are my daily routines?
- How do I talk?
- How do I dress?

- What do I do to take care of myself?
- What kind of conversations do I have?
- What do I value?
- What am I grateful for?

As you stop to reflect on your life up to this point, what do you recognize as behaviors, thoughts, and actions that have brought what you desire into your life? It is also useful to acknowledge what conduct, views, and activities have negated you having what you want.

Continue to employ all that works and be willing to let go of thoughts, beliefs, and actions that don't assist you in evolving to your highest level of living. Practice honing your visualization skills. This is one of the most powerful ways I know to manifest what you want in your life.

Chapter Four

So Help Me, God

"Let us not become weary in doing good, for at the proper time we will reap a harvest if we do not give up."
— Galatians 6:9

SUMMERTIME BROUGHT WITH it long and rigorous days. If we weren't on tractors tending to the land, we were cutting hay and stockpiling food for our cattle to survive the winter. The month of July was especially grueling because it was when we harvested wheat.

A burgeoning wheat crop was imperative because it not only put food on the table; it also afforded us the ability to farm for another year. A fruitful harvest was not guaranteed. Every year at this time we had a date with destiny, and Mother Nature played a critical role in the outcome of what the harvest season would yield—if anything.

The date was June 3, 1968. I stood on a chair next to George at the south-facing window in our small, humble kitchen. He was thirty-eight. I was seven. The sky was the color of Midnight Blue in the sixty-four-count Crayola® crayon box. We watched together as hailstones the size of softballs fully mowed down the amber waves of grain that had grown to waist-tall, plump, and plumb-full of wheat kernels.

We were broke, and I was brokenhearted. George had tears in his eyes, and my little head thought, *there must have been something I could have done to prevent this from happening.* After all, I carried a rosary in the front, right pocket of my blue jeans, and said the rosary EVERY. SINGLE. DAY. When hail clouds reared their ugly head, which was all too frequent, I never stopped praying until those clouds passed.

I remember climbing on that chair, holding my rosary in my hand to look out the kitchen window that day. The smell in the air was that of freshly cut hay. But, in reality, it was the smell of a completely destroyed wheat crop we couldn't afford to lose. I stepped down from the chair to seek refuge somewhere in our tiny house. Sadness rushed to every cell in my body, and guilt set up shop in my head as I struggled to understand the horrible loss that I had just witnessed.

It was late afternoon and I needed to talk to God right then. You see, God sat at the foot of my bed every night, and we talked. He was a handsome and wise old fella, with an astonishingly thick head of silver hair and a beard to match. He was my friend. My go-to guy. He kept me safe. We chatted about a lot of things. His voice was always thunderous yet reasonable. However, today was different.

I had an emergency situation that needed His attention immediately. I cannot recall with any specificity how our conversation went, except I was mad as hell. How could He let this happen to us? We were poor, and I was scared. He was supposed to be my friend, my protector. He was the all-knowing dude with all the power.

Would it have been any hair off His chest to have protected all us farmers from this slaughter? But—God somehow convinced me to keep the faith, to believe and trust in Him. Even though it didn't seem like it, He would keep me out of the ditch, so to speak. So, I kept saying the rosary. Every single day.

The next morning, George loaded my two brothers and me into our Ford pickup, and we made the nine-mile journey into Wray, Colorado.

Wray was our small town. Our rural community, comprised of roughly 1,900 people—around 750 families—most of whom were farmers or ranchers. As with most small towns, Main Street was a big deal.

Main Street in Wray was a whopping three blocks long. Those blocks housed the likes of the Rexall Drug Store, Duckwalls, Wray Lumber, Amos Jewelry, and the *Wray Gazette*, as well as a post office, barber shop, bakery, and, of course, the pool hall. The day after the hailstorm massacre, Main Street was eerie and solemn. The owner of the drugstore had gathered some of the hailstones and put them in the freezer alongside the vanilla, chocolate, and strawberry ice cream in his shop.

The lid of the freezer would get lifted to show visitors the weapons of mass destruction that had devastated so many families and their livelihood just hours before. George had saved a few, too. Those massive chunks of perfectly rounded ice occupied our freezer as if they were the grand prize of some time-honored competition. I disdained the sight of the damn things and couldn't wait until something more useful took their place.

So, that's how it went as a farmer. We never knew if all our hard work would pay off or not. But it is the chance you take when you farm. It taught me that perseverance was a prerequisite to a lifestyle of making a living off the land. There was a rhythm to the days on the farm, no matter the season.

Although we didn't even turn a combine on during what would have been harvesttime in 1968, most other years we did. It was the income from my mom being a nurse that helped us squeak by during unfruitful farming years. As a kid, I didn't know just how poor we were. I didn't have a reference for what that meant except that I was an eyewitness to the despair that a hailstorm could bring to my family.

My whole life, I had worn my older brother's hand-me-downs. I didn't have a concept of what it meant to go on a family vacation every year. My brothers and I had the vastness of the great outdoors as our unlimited source for exploration and entertainment. As far as we were concerned, we had everything we needed. Sometimes, it is what you don't know that is the ultimate blessing.

Until I was old enough to drive a wheat truck, I would ride along on the combine, or one of the trucks, as the wheat was hauled off to be stored in steel bins or the elevator in town.

Each morning I would watch the guys who operated the combines and trucks as they inspected their machine, checked the oil, and greased them up for the day ahead. I paid close attention to how the driver tucked in next to the combine and drove alongside it as the wheat was moved from the combine into the truck box.

I learned how to use an auger. I studied how to use the hoist on the wheat truck. I learned how to scoop the corners out of the back of the uplifted truck bed, ensuring all the grain made it to its final destination. I helped the driver place the tarp over the top of the wheat so it wouldn't blow out of the back of the truck on the way to the elevator.

When we arrived at the elevator, I paid close attention to where the truck was positioned on the massive scale so that it could be weighed before and after it was emptied. I observed as the elevator worker drove a probe deep into the load of wheat on the truck and pulled a sample that would be used to test the moisture level and weight of the grain.

So many jobs I paid close attention to, learning—then doing—all these physically and mentally challenging jobs. I didn't think about it at the time, but growing up on the farm was like getting a master's degree in auto mechanics, animal husbandry, and agriculture—all at the same time via on-the-job training from the school of hard knocks.

Pause and Reflect: Make a Contribution

Looking back on my childhood, I realize that there were so many unknowns. But, the one thing that I did know for sure was, I wanted to contribute to our family. I didn't want to be a burden or add to the anguish of the uncertain days of farming. The only way I knew how to do that was to learn how to be helpful in some way. It made me feel good to lend a hand.

I have come to discover that the natural, yet unclaimed wisdom that I had as a child holds valuable acumen and insights even in the dynamic and tumultuous world that we live in today. Here are a few:

1. There is freedom in the unknown. As a child, not knowing allowed me to trust. I didn't know enough to overthink anything. I merely took matters as they came and participated in the unfolding of events without the need to control. As an adult, I remind myself of this often. Let things be. Let what wants to come, come, and let what wants to go, go.

2. I always had all that I needed. Even when I was hungry, I had God. How smart is that? Knowing that the Divine Source will take care of everything. There is no need for grasping, or ownership, or attachment. I have found that when I surrender to the fact that I no longer "need" anything, then I can have everything, and when I stop attempting to make things happen, that anything can.

3. Contributing to the good of the whole matters. Even though I couldn't impact the financial situation of our family, I could be a useful member of the team. I believe that one of the biggest reasons that people are unhappy in our modern culture is because they have failed to embrace the importance of adding value and being of service to those around them. If you want to rock your world, rock someone else's first.

Chapter Five

OFF TO SCHOOL

"There's no way in hell I would have walked out of my childhood whole without my daily chats with God."
— Annie M. Fonte

ONCE WE WERE old enough to go to school, my brothers and I would get on a bus each morning at 7:15 am. The driver was our Uncle Bob. Almost every kid who rode the bus with us called him "Uncle Bob" because we did. He was a calm and likable guy who managed to keep a bunch of farm kids in reasonably good order as we traveled over the same roads each day on our way to school.

Maintaining discipline was no easy task, especially since the boy passengers had a lot of pent-up energy and were hellions. I was shy and kept to myself, but not my brothers. They led the charge—there was never a dull moment. But it was all good, clean fun, and Uncle Bob let the boys be boys. My brothers tell stories to this day of the shenanigans that happened on that twenty-mile bus ride each day.

I was a good student all through grade school and high school. I enjoyed learning, but I was not a gifted or a natural scholar. I had to work to get good grades, which I did. I also read a lot. I didn't know hardly anything about what was possible outside of farm life, but I imagined there was major promise beyond the confines of the small world into which I was born.

I would go to the little library in my school and check out books about presidents. My fifth-grade logic led me to believe that presidents were successful people, and surely I could learn about what existed in the world if I studied these famous men. The more I read, the more encouraged I was that one day, I could go to faraway places and do big things if I wanted to.

During the school year, my brothers and I would have to get the chores done before the bus came to cart us off to the red brick buildings where we went to learn things.

That same bus would drop us back off at the farm in the late afternoon. We would change into our work clothes and carry out our evening responsibilities before eating dinner. I would immediately do my homework after dinner. My brothers? Not so much. Both of them, brilliant in their own way, did not have any appreciation or desire to excel through the margins of the school curriculum.

I wanted to get my schoolwork done as quickly as possible, because then I could sit quietly in my bedroom—by myself—and read, write, or draw. Something was comforting to me about this quiet time. I needed this time to rejuvenate myself, and I felt safe in my little corner of our tiny, modest home. I still have a daily practice of peaceful reflection.

It was during these hours of solitude at the end of each day that I had my talks with God. We talked about all kinds of things. I would tell Him about my day at school and what I'd learned. I would ask for His help when I felt worried or uncertain. I requested that He talk to me until I fell asleep, especially when I was hungry.

And, I pleaded with Him to see what He could do about having the tooth fairy leave me some money when I lost a tooth. Now and then, a nickel or dime would replace my little tooth, but most of the time—after a few days—I would remove my tooth from under my pillow and put it in a special, small box where I kept some other things that I treasured, including my previously lost teeth.

I cherished my chats with God. It gave me something to look forward to, and someone to rely on during those unsure days of my childhood. My admiration for God and my desire to have Him in my life has never changed. As I grew older, I continued to go to church and say the rosary with regularity, always having esteem for the role that divinity played in my being.

It wasn't until I chose to revamp my life that I came to realize that I wasn't separate from God. His divineness existed inside of me, and I had access to Him at any time, no matter the time of day or the circumstances. We are one together, as long as I choose that for myself. If I experience what feels like disconnection from Him, it's because I've allowed my ego a seat at the table.

Three's a crowd in these situations. There is no room for me, ego, and God to occupy the same space, at the same time. It happens every time I start thinking, instead of being. I have come to know that operating from ego is fear-based and a sure way to land in the ditch of despair.

So, as long as I select God, my journey is smooth, effortless, and peaceful. It is love-based, and I highly recommend it.

Chapter Six

———∼∽∼———

THE PISSING CONTEST

"Don't pray for an easy life, pray for the strength to endure a difficult one."

— Bruce Lee

DURING THE SUMMERS, my brothers and I shared the stock tanks with our cattle, which served as their watering hole and our swimming pool. At some point, we physically outgrew the practicality of the size and shallowness of these water vessels. Going to the public pool in town was a rare but thrilling treat. That great, big pool gave us room to splash around with other kids and hone our swimming skills.

None of us took lessons to learn how to swim—we just watched the kids who had and copied what they did. The pool had a shallow end and a deep end, separated by a bright, blue and white, floating rope. The rite of passage into the deep end entailed swimming the width of the pool twice.

I practiced in the shallow end until I thought I could pass the test, then walked up to a lifeguard and told her I was ready. I combined my underwater swimming skills with the dog paddle and managed to navigate the requisite distance without drowning. I loved these occasional breaks in the lengthy, arduous days on the farm.

One day, George dropped us off at the pool while he took care of business around town. He said he'd be back to get us in two hours. I went to the girl's locker room to change into my bathing suit (which was my mom's one-piece, with built-in, padded bra cups). Of course, in a perfect world, I would've preferred swimwear of my own, but we couldn't afford it.

I was twelve, so you can imagine the fashion statement I made as I stepped out onto the crowded pool deck, sporting a grown woman's bathing suit, coupled with a glaringly obvious farmer's tan. It didn't take long for the city kids—who spent every day at the pool—to start taunting and teasing me.

I was embarrassed and ashamed. I went back to the locker room, changed back into my blue jeans, t-shirt, and cowboy boots. For the next two hours, I sat on the steps waiting for George, while my brothers swam with the city kids. That was the last time I went to town to swim that summer.

PAUSE AND REFLECT: A SWIMWEAR MOMENT

It is likely that it wasn't wearing your mom's one-piece swimming suit that brought on taunting by others at some point in your youth. Very few of us will escape some form of jeering from another in our life. It is just how it goes. It was in this moment of vulnerability that I discovered that individuality—simply being me—held the possibility of danger.

It is times like this that invite the imagination to engage in the rawness of the shallow perceptions of people who don't know us or care about us. They themselves are merely struggling to survive, to keep their head above the waters of self-discovery, and building healthy self-acceptance.

Unfortunately, as young children, we don't have the ability to gracefully handle the tactless teasing that others bestow upon us. Often, we are too ashamed to tell our parents or other adults who might be able to help us. Instead, we keep our feelings of unworthiness stored deep inside where we hold disgrace.

We cannot access the enlightenment that we were born with because layers of doubt and uncertainty have pushed it to a place within us that is unreachable. As adults, it is essential to work this out. Otherwise, we will trek through big chunks of our lives carrying around pointless and heavy baggage like anger, resentment, unworthiness, self-doubt, and fear—none of which are useful to us or inspiring to others.

Whatever your swimwear moments are, now is the time to unchain yourself from them. Free yourself from the weight of anything in your past that is keeping you from being your best self. There is no good reason to hold on to situations or events that you can no longer save because the price of what is dying inside of you is too high.

It isn't okay to function externally while fighting to deaden the pain inside of you. Rewrite the story in a way that impassions you and others to live the shit out of life. Believe that life happens for you—because it does. And then, when you get this all sorted out for yourself, help a kid.

If you are a parent, be present enough in your child's life to recognize when they are grappling with the stuff that they encounter in their day. Listen deeply and be available when they need you. Teach them to invite the kid sitting by themselves in the school cafeteria to join them for lunch. Explain to them that being a bully or being bullied isn't acceptable, which is different than a well-deserved ass-kicking.

Help them to understand that most people are "bullies" or "mean girls" because they are afraid and lack self-esteem. Impart to them the significance of being authentic and that it is better to be who they are than to "fit in." Most importantly, be a good example for them.

Let who you are being in the world, as well as your words and your actions, set an example. Instill in them goodness and confidence and compassion. If you are not a parent but an adult who has interaction with and potential impact on a child or children, do the same.

CITY KIDS COME TO THE FARM

As luck would have it, my parents were friends with some of the city kids' parents.

Occasionally, the families would come to the farm to visit. While the parents chatted, played cards, and had a few cocktails, my brothers and I would entertain the city crew. This is where being a farm kid came in very handy. When Mike, Dan, and I weren't doing farmwork, we spent our free time cooking up ways to amuse ourselves.

These tactics included but were not limited to, shooting BB guns at each other, playing chicken with jackknives and pitchforks, and blowing things up with M-80 firecrackers. This clearly gave us plenty of ruses at the ready to share with the unknowing and unprepared city slickers.

One of our favorite tricks was the pissing contest. We would get all the boys—including my brothers—to line up about five feet from a live electric fence. The young men who could pee far enough to hit the thin charged wire were the esteemed "winners" of the challenge.

Of course, my brothers never won because they knew the shocking cost of victory. You can imagine the satisfactory outcome of watching the city folk pee all over themselves, getting zapped by the electric wire. Out of embarrassment, they never told their parents, all while learning a valuable lesson about making fun of us tough country kids' ill-fitting swimsuits, farmer's tans and all.

Occurrences like these reinforced my gratitude for being raised on a farm. It instilled an appreciation of a hard day's work. The more I sat on a tractor and churned the earth, the more I came to love and respect the land. I was glad I was a farm kid and not a city kid.

I was happy to get up each morning with a purpose and lay my head on my pillow each night knowing I had accomplished something. I understood at a very young age the significance of contributing to our family and being a reliable member of our clan. I noticed the resolve my brothers and I had versus our friends and classmates who did not live on a farm.

Chapter Seven

WHEN THE COWS COME MARCHING IN

"Until one has loved an animal, a part of one's soul remains unawakened."

— Anatole France

EACH YEAR, SUMMER would gracefully bow out, giving the stage to fall and winter. Although I've never been fond of the limited hours of daylight that come with winter's arrival, I recognized at a young age that the rest and solace of those days were a welcome and needed change of pace from the rigors of summer.

The tractors and other farm equipment enjoyed a well-deserved respite, while the cattle stepped into the spotlight. George was a brilliant cattleman and taught us the importance of taking good care of our herd. We had a decent amount of pastureland where we grazed our cattle during the spring and summer months.

However, before the snow started to fall, we would have to move them all to the corrals and lean-tos we had constructed close to our house. Winter was also the calving season for us. Calving is a 24/7 activity. The expectant moms must be checked on every couple of hours, around the clock, to ensure a safe and trouble-free birth.

We would put plenty of straw down under the roofs of the shelters, which would serve as bedding for the cows to deliver their babies. Most of the mature cows lie down and push out a new calf, usually without help. A new calf enters the world front-feet first and weighs between sixty and seventy pounds.

If the calf is bigger than seventy pounds, or if anything other than the front feet try to come out first, things can get dicey pretty quick. As long as it appears that a cow is going through typical labor, it's best to leave her alone. Once a cow goes into labor, she should give birth within two to three hours.

However, if she seems to be struggling and her effort to give birth isn't progressing, then it's time to step in and help. It's always nice to have the assistance of a vet during these rare but challenging times, especially if the calf is in an abnormal position, or if the cow has a twisted uterus.

We were fortunate to have a vet who lived reasonably close to us, so most of the time he was able to get to us, and our strained cows, to assist in a successful birth. On the few occasions he couldn't make it, we were able to take matters into our own hands. If the calf's front feet were showing and we could determine its head was in the right position, we would aid in the delivery.

I was always an eager participant in pulling calves because I so badly wanted them and their mamas to be okay. I just loved those babies. Because my hands were small and agile, I was often the one who would place the pull-chain on the front feet. The task was a messy job because there was always blood, manure, and amniotic fluid flowing freely.

The chain looked similar to a dog's choke collar, but it had handles at the end that were used to get leverage to pull the calf through the birth canal. When the baby arrives, it is soaking wet, and it's crucial the mama quickly starts to lick it with her rough tongue to help stimulate the baby to take its first breath and get dry. Most of the time the calf is standing and nursing within an hour or two.

This is vital because a dry baby with a full tummy can withstand a surprising amount of cold. I think I was about five years old when I watched the vet and my dad pull a calf for the first time. I was in awe of the whole event. It was astonishing to me that this slimy, wet, and wobbly creature came out of its mom's belly. Amazing.

From that point on, I was in. I wanted to be there every single time a new baby needed help being born. I'm happy to report that during all my years on the farm, only a handful of babies or mama cows perished during calving season, but not without unyielding effort on our part to keep this from happening.

Each casualty ushered in immense sorrow to my young and impressionable heart. I didn't realize it at the time, but witnessing how fragile life can be at such a tender age brought with it an appreciation of the cycle of life, both in the human race and the animal kingdom. Each time a baby or mama died, I would caress its lifeless body and close its eyes. Then, I would pull my rosary from my right front pocket and say a prayer for it.

In addition to the hourly inspections on the soon-to-be moms, the cattle needed to be fed twice a day during the cold and blustery days of the Colorado winters. My brothers, our dad, and I would layer up, covering every inch of our bodies with some form of protection against the blistering wind and breathtaking cold temperatures. We would head out to the herd, each doing our part to get food for the cows in the feed bunks and make sure the water tanks hadn't iced over.

Daunting blizzards were often the norm on the vast and flat plains surrounding the farm, sometimes bringing twenty inches or more of snow. It was not unusual for snow drifts to peak at eight to ten feet, which added extra trials to tending to the animals.

I remember one winter when, square in the middle of a blinding blizzard as we armored up to feed the cattle, my mom tied bedsheets together to act as a tether between the house and the corral. We counted on that lifeline for a safe return to the house once we completed our chores.

These same blizzards would down the power lines that provided electricity to the widespread farmhouses—ours included. We would go for days with no electricity, which meant no heat, no cooking, and no lights. We did our best to stay warm and entertain ourselves in the hours between our outside responsibilities.

I would read during the day and play cards with my brothers at night by candlelight. When I was a junior in high school, George was able to buy a generator, which allowed us to cook, keep the refrigerator and freezer operating, run the heater periodically, and have a few lights on at night. For me, this was more than a blessing; it was a luxury. For the first time in my life, getting through the harshest of the four seasons was a little more comfortable.

I considered spring to be the most applauded time of year. The thaw from the unforgiving winter commenced, and signs of renewed life popped up as the grass got greener, flowers began to bloom, and the days grew longer and warmer—all of which was an improvement from the previous five months.

We moved the cows and their young babies back to pastureland, where they would freely graze and enjoy having expansive acres to roam over and relax. George and I would spend hours driving along the miles of fence line, making repairs where necessary to ensure the cows stayed within the precincts of our property. We would perform required maintenance on the windmill, making sure it would efficiently pump water into the stock tank for the cattle.

The tractors and other farm equipment came out from their wintertime siesta and underwent rigorous inspections, maintenance, and repair, in preparation for the upcoming farming term. Irrespective of the season, there was always something to do on the farm. I loved almost everything about it. Every year I learned more and was more capable of handling many of these tasks on my own.

KEEP YOUR ASS IN THE SADDLE

Chapter Eight

～❧～

DANGEROUS BUSINESS

"It's a dangerous business, going out of your door. You step onto the road, and if you don't keep your feet, there's no telling where you might be swept off to."
— *The Fellowship of the Ring*

GROWING UP ON a farm offers abundant chances to get in precarious situations. I remember one day, we were in the field with George, too young to operate the equipment on our own. It was late summer when one uses a piece of equipment called a disc to start the process of turning under the post-harvest stubble that remains after cutting the wheat.

We came upon an electric fence with high weeds growing underneath it. Weeds are one of a farmer's most detested enemies, and we went to great lengths to ensure their demise. George stopped the tractor and told us to get off to help him. He lifted Dan onto his shoulders.

He told Mike and me to grab the electric fence wire and hand it to him so he could pass it along to Dan, who would then hammer the wire to the high-wire pole, allowing George to make a swipe under the fence line and take out all the weeds. As George handed the wire to Dan, the tension was powerful enough to pull Dan off balance, which, in turn, drew George off balance and launched Dan squarely toward the disc.

As Mike and I saw this happening, we tackled George and pushed him into the ditch, most likely saving Dan's life. The blades on the disc are so sharp that, had any part of Dan's body come in contact with the razorlike edges, the outcome would have been deadly.

Neither George nor Dan knew what happened as they flew into the ditch. It was when they got up and collected themselves that they both realized they had narrowly escaped great harm, possibly even death.

Once the dust settled, so to speak, George, without saying a word moved the equipment away from the fence line, and we did a "take two" on hiking the wire out of the way, allowing George to make a broad swipe with the disc beneath the hiked fence. So the weeds met their final ruin, and we all assumed our usual positions on the tractor and carried on with the day.

The disc played a starring role in another episode of "farm accidents do happen." Each fall, as we prepared to put our equipment in storage, we would oil the blades of the disc to keep it from rusting during the harsh winter months. This maintenance process entailed wrapping old rags around a two-by-four secured with twine.

We would then fill a five-gallon bucket with diesel oil. As one person turned the blades of the disc, the other would use the stick that had been dipped in the oil to lubricate the individual metal circles on this big piece of farm equipment. One warm fall day, when I was ten and Dan was seven, George sent us to a field about two miles from the house where the disc sat, ready for our oiling skills.

We got all set up and started our task. Dan, with his hands tucked into thick leather gloves, was the turner, and I was the oiler. Only a few minutes into our project, Dan pulled his gloved hands away from the disc, and I looked to see why he had stopped his duty. I watched as he pulled off the gloves and held his profusely bleeding hand in the air.

He had caught his finger on one of the razor-sharp parts of the disc, and it was dangling by a thin piece of skin. We agreed that we needed to jump in the pickup and drive home so that George could get us to the hospital. So, there we were, me in the driver's seat, so shaken up by the fact we had managed to cut Dan's finger all but off, and him, in the passenger's seat, holding his hand over a coffee can full of nails, catching the stream of blood gushing from his finger.

I was doing my best to maintain my composure, but my leg was trembling so much I could barely hold my foot on the gas pedal. Dan kept telling me to speed it up, and I kept telling him I couldn't go over my speed limit, which was thirty-five mph at the time.

When we pulled into the yard, George jumped off the tractor wanting to know why we were back so soon. Then he saw Dan get out of the truck—a bloody mess. I talked as fast as I could to explain what happened while George took Dan in the house to clean him up a bit before we all got in the car to drive to the hospital. George was both concerned and pissed.

A cut-off finger had really thrown a wrench into the day. In the meantime, nine miles away, my mom received a phone call from the highway patrol informing the hospital that a parent was bringing a youngster in who was involved in a farm accident. She readied the staff and got the emergency room set up. Ten minutes later, she looked up and there we were: George, Dan, and me, rushing down the hallway of the hospital.

The injured child was her very own. She swiftly escorted George and Dan to the ER, where she assisted the surgeon in sewing Dan's finger back on. The undertaking was not easy, given the fact that the blade had sliced through tendon and bone. George told me to sit on the front steps of the hospital and wait, so I did. I sat there in my blue jeans, cowboy boots, and a t-shirt with diesel oil all over it.

I sat there for hours, saying the rosary and praying that the brother I loved so much would be okay. I rode home with my mom from the hospital because, by the time they had patched Dan up, her shift was over. Exhausted from the unforeseen activities of the day, we all went to sleep.

The next morning, I got in the pickup with George and went back to the scene of the crime to finish oiling the disc. He drove, and we managed to return home with all of our body parts intact. My mom went back to the hospital to serve those in need, never knowing who might walk through the door.

Chapter Nine

4-H

"A lot of groups go out there and talk about it. We go out there and actually do it."

— 4-H, "Join the Revolution
of Responsibility" poster

WHEN I WAS eight years old, I was old enough to be a member of 4-H. Participating in this program is something that I wanted to do. My parents didn't force me to be in the club, and they were supportive of my projects and activities. Neither of my brothers were ever members. The meetings and structure and project requirements were too stifling for their wild-at-heart natures.

4-H is a youth development program that offers young kids the opportunity to develop leadership skills by participating in curriculums ranging from engineering and technology to plant and animal sciences.

The organization's pledge is: "I pledge my HEAD to clearer thinking, my HEART to greater loyalty, my HANDS to larger service, and my HEALTH to better living, for my club, my community, my country, and my world." Hence, the 4-Hs. I chose sewing and beef-fattening as my undertakings for the five years that I took part in 4-H.

Beef-fattening required that I pick a young steer to take care of, keep records of how much I was feeding him and the costs, prepare him to be sold, and show him during the county fair, which was in the summer each year. These animals became big, loving pets.

I would train them to be haltered and led in a precise fashion, required by the show judges. My first steer was my favorite. His name was Snowflake. He was white with a sprinkle of black speckles throughout his coat—a real show-stopper. I spent hours with him.

I would groom him, talk to him, and love him as much as I could. It got to the point where he would let me lie on his back, and he would follow me anywhere, even without his halter and lead rope. Beef-fattening prizes are based on how much weight the animal gained from the first day in your care to the weigh-in day at the fair.

My sweet Snowflake put on an average of 2.73 pounds per day. That was good enough to secure a fourth-place ribbon. There was nothing like a fattened-up steer to capture the attention of a willing buyer. The sad part was saying good-bye to this pet you had become so attached to over the previous months.

They were going to the buyer to be slain, then eaten, part by part. Even though I knew all of this going in, it was never fun to leave the fair with only a halter in your hand and an empty place in your heart. But that was all part of the cycle of life that being a farm girl taught me.

I continued to partake in beef-fattening for four more years, each time walking away with tears in my eyes and a stiff upper lip, knowing I had loved my steer with my whole heart. I enjoyed my sewing projects, mostly because I learned the value of precision and being attentive to the fine points that make the most significant difference as a seamstress, and in life.

My sewing teacher was patient, and I was a willing student and a stickler for details. Over the years I crafted a skirt with an elastic waistband, a plaid jacket, and a couple of pantsuits, one of which received

Grand Champion Prize recognition. Sewing was fun, and I liked creating something from nothing.

The most challenging part of the sewing endeavors was the requirement to model your outfit in front of a panel of judges. This meant stepping onto a stage donning the garment that you had spent months stitching together and going through the motions of hitting three separate marks that had been placed on the floor with masking tape.

The idea was to walk to each "X" and with as much grace as you could muster, do a quarter turn to the right, then to the left, finished off with a 180-degree turn, which would allow the judges to view all angles of your ensemble. One of the most dreaded days of my life every year for four years was having to pace and twirl my way across that stage.

Then, 4-H gave way to sports when I started high school. I had to pick one or the other, and my choice was, hands down, being an athlete.

You do what you have to do

Once my brothers and I started participating in sports, we stopped taking the bus to school and started driving ourselves.

None of us were legally old enough to transport ourselves to school each day, but, as the saying goes, *"Necessity is the mother of invention."* George was able to get clearance from the highway patrol that would permit us to drive directly to and from school so we could stay after classes to participate in each of our sport practice sessions.

As big of a deal this might have been for other kids our age, for us, it was a nonevent. We all started driving at such a young age, we would argue about who had to drive to and from school each day. We finally settled on a weekly schedule. Each of us would take our turn at the wheel for an entire week, then get two weeks off.

Mike was fourteen, I was thirteen, and Dan was ten when we started carting ourselves back and forth from the farm to the halls of knowledge and after-school sports programs. It all worked out for the best. My brothers and I could be involved in the sports we loved, and it lifted restrictions and inconveniences from our parents' work schedules.

You see, farming doesn't wait for you. It doesn't take a break so your dad can take you to school or come and get you at the end of the day. There is no time for that. Every minute counts, and accomplishing what needs to be done is often a race against the clock. And our mom had to work. Her income was vital to our existence.

A steady income is not a guarantee that comes with farming. I remember some very lean years growing up. There were times when my parents would skip a meal so my brothers and I could have something to eat. Not a full meal, but a little bit of nourishment was better than nothing.

I would often wear my older brother's clothes, or I would wear my clothes way past a proper fit. Most of the time I was not aware of the meager life we led until a kid at school would make fun of me because my pants were way too short or I dressed like a boy. And so, I would go home and talk to God. He never made fun of me.

Chapter Ten

ANOREXIA

*"You deserve peace, love, happiness and all that your heart desires.
Don't let anyone control your life and take away those things."*
— Sonya Parker

ONCE WE ENTERED our teenage years, George's belt took a back seat to a less violent form of manipulation: verbal abuse. As a young girl, I spent a lot of time with George, and I wanted to please him. I did so with good grades, admirable behavior, and being an extremely hard worker around the farm.

George and I would go fishing together. He helped me with my 4-H steers; we went coyote hunting, target shooting, and a handful of other unique father/daughter bonding activities. Every now and then he would treat me to a banana split after school. I enjoyed and appreciated all of these gestures but realize now it was all part of his need to control and be admired.

When I started high school and began playing sports, our relationship changed. George's self-absorbed habit of giving unsolicited advice highlighted his view of his superior knowledge and insights. Also, he wanted me to be an impressive athlete so he could be the center of attention because "he was my dad."

To his credit, he hardly ever missed one of my games or track meets. I think my parents were proud of my brothers and me. However, George always wanted to analyze us. He would sit me down at the kitchen table, and—although he was happy with the victories—he continually critiqued how I played.

He was imposing and controlling, but I was of an age that, even though he seemed overbearing, I didn't have the maturity to understand the narcissistic part of his personality. As the discomfort of his mannerisms mounted, I yearned for command of my own life.

So, in the only way I knew how at the time, I took charge of the one thing he couldn't dominate: what I ate. I wasn't overweight or even concerned about my weight, but I could take the reins and secure a little power I so desperately desired. I started limiting my caloric intake and upping my workouts, even beyond the hardcore practice and conditioning regimes my sports required.

My plan worked well for a while. As the pounds (which I couldn't afford to lose) melted away from my already lean physique, I felt better, I played better, and in my mind—I was in charge. George was oblivious to the change in my stature because the level of my performance was noticeably rising.

For the first time in a long time, the post-game assessments were short and sweet. However—as it goes with most bad ideas—the negatives outweighed the positives. Several months into this power-grab scheme, I weighed in at ninety-eight pounds, compromising (to say the least) my 5'6" frame.

I remember coming home from basketball practice one night, hungry. I ate a handful of lettuce with nothing on it and drank a glass of water. I then went to my room to do my extended workout, and about ten minutes in, I went to the bathroom and threw up my robust meal of lettuce with the water chaser. That was the moment I knew that I was in trouble.

My half-baked notion of being large-and-in-charge of my life met its demise. There I was, exposed, and atrophied. My body was lonely for love and acceptance. I had allowed George's narcissism to escort me straight to the altar of anorexia. I was scared, and I knew I needed help.

I went to my mom and told her I was concerned I might have an ulcer and asked for her help, not wanting to admit my eating disorder. Digging out of the clutches of anorexia isn't easy. I had grown accustomed to my slight stature, and I actually liked how I felt; not the throwing up part, but for me, there was some measure of satisfaction in being light and lean.

I also liked how I looked. However, I now realize that I had a distorted perception of weight, which is not uncommon for a person wrestling with an eating disorder. Food was not my challenge, and over time, I was able to pack on a few pounds that got me out of the danger zone. The real challenge was that I didn't have enough tools in my toolbox to cope with the emotional rollercoaster ride of living with a man who, despite his best efforts, was not cut out to be a dad.

PAUSE AND REFLECT: YOU ARE WORTHY. BELIEVE IT.

As I look back on this time, it is heartbreaking to know that there was a young girl quietly endeavoring to contain the sorrow of feeling unworthy; and she was me. I was a young girl who could not access the voice of compassion in my own heart. How ironic it is that it took the death of George for the glow of enlightenment to knock gently on the door of my soul, requesting entrance to a place that had long been dark in its absence.

For years I had drowned out the holiness and wisdom of the voice of my heart and soul. Knowing this now, I listen deeply to this voice. The feel and quality of my life are better, and each day I appreciate how precious life is. I urge you to do the same. Allow yourself the freedom to see through the veils of illusion that you have grasped onto as reality.

Whatever those situations are that have caused you to let unworthiness seep into your being, let them go. Do not spend one more minute in circumstances that squander your specialness or deplete your spirit. Trust in the beauty and sureness of your own soul. Do this for yourself and start right now. Listen deeply to your own knowingness and uncage your essence.

Chapter Eleven

―――⚬∿∿⚬―――

ATHLETICS

"Be humble. Be hungry. And always be the hardest worker in the room."

— Dwayne "The Rock" Johnson

ALL THROUGH HIGH school, I participated in volleyball, basketball, and track. My brothers were wrestlers and football players. It is important to acknowledge that my parents hardly ever missed a game. They went to great lengths to arrange their schedules to watch us play sports.

I was fortunate to play volleyball and basketball for a young, brave, and determined coach who took a bunch of wholesome young girls from a little town in the middle of nowhere and made a bit of history. It was 1975, and I was a freshman in high school.

Let's back up for a second. In 1972, Richard Nixon signed Title IX into law. The passing of this legislation meant the beginning of organized sports programs for females in high school and college. Before this, the only option for athletic girls was the Girls Athletic Association, which—although important—was limited, at best.

In 1974, it was announced there would be a state volleyball and basketball tournament for girls in the state of Colorado. The first girls state volleyball competition was in 1975, followed by basketball in 1976. Our tiny-but-mighty team, the Wray Eagles, made our way to the basketball tournament—and won. In fact, not only did we win the first year, we were the state champions for the following three years.

I graduated in 1978, so I was on a championship team my entire high school basketball career. Some of us were farm kids; others were daughters of local business owners and school teachers. Some of us were fast, some tall, some had a little more talent than others, but we all had one thing in common: heart. Okay, two things: drive and heart. We believed we could beat any team. And we did.

We were warriors on the court and ladies off the court. Our coach made sure of that. We practiced hard and often. We had a daily conditioning schedule that was terrifying, but, when we stepped onto that court, we were beyond ready, and a major threat to our opponents.

Today—almost four decades later—I still reflect on those memories and the components it took to make us the time-honored team we were. Truly, the elements we practiced to become athletic successes were no different than what it takes to build time-honored companies, relationships, friendships, or lives. Simply put: if you go all-in, work your ass off, listen, and do what it takes, you will not lose.

The following is an excerpt from a speech given by Theodore Roosevelt on April 23, 1910, in Paris, France:

> *It is not the critic who counts, not the man who points out how the strong man stumbles, or where the doer of deeds could have done them better. The credit belongs to the man in the arena, whose face is marred by dust and sweat and blood, who strives valiantly ... who knows great enthusiasms, the great devotions; who spends himself in a worthy cause, who at the best knows in the end the triumph of high achievement, and who, at worst, if he fails, at least he fails while daring greatly, so that his place shall never be with*

those cold and timid souls who have never known neither victory or defeat.

Roosevelt's passage described our team perfectly. All of us courageously stepped into the arena. There was sweat and blood; there was enthusiasm and devotion; and there was victory and high achievement. Many of those wholesome young girls went on to become remarkable women, and our coach was inducted into the Coaches Hall of Fame.

They hold honorable positions and serve noble roles in the world. They were champions then, and they are champions now. So, what is my historical perspective? Some things change, and some remain the same. What's changed? We're all a little older and, hopefully, a little wiser.

We are scattered throughout this great country, with families and vocations and a bag full of experiences. The world moves a lot faster today than it did back then, and technology has made this fast-paced world a lot smaller. One could debate the pluses and minuses of such change.

But, more importantly, what remains the same—at least for me—was being a part of that mighty little team with a potent coach who left an indelible mark on me. I often reflect back to all the practices, the bus rides, the games, the celebrated wins, and I smile. I am proud. I am grateful. And sometimes I miss the "good ole days."

But regardless of how much time passes, it is a true honor to have been one of those girls, learning so much at such an impressionable age, together and under such great leadership. Our dominant little team won a lot. Almost always. As a sophomore, I made the varsity team and chose #20 as my uniform number. Our team won the first state championship, and I was recognized as the MVP of the tournament wearing that number. #20 meant a lot to me. #20 hung in every closet I had until 2007, when it perished when my home burned down.

As a basketball player, I was decent on offense, but a demon on defense. I would practice on my own, shooting baskets for hours—sometimes well into the night—with only the yard light as my companion.

I measured five feet six inches tall. My height was sufficient to be a setter on the volleyball team. The trouble was, I didn't want to be a setter. I wanted to be a hitter. There was something about smashing the shit out of a volleyball that I loved, but when you are only 5'6" you had to be capable of jumping if you wanted to be a hitter.

So, here is what I did: I went out to the field by our house, took a shovel, and dug a hole. When the chasm got deep enough, I would jump in and out of that hole until I could do it with confidence and ease. Then, I dug deeper. I kept doing this until I couldn't jump out anymore.

I managed to increase my vertical jump to thirty-four inches, achieving my goal of hitting the shit out of volleyballs. When I wasn't shooting baskets or jumping out of my hole in the ground, I would get on my John Deere ten-speed bike and ride for miles on the gravel roads that made up the massive grid of connection between the tens of thousands of acres of farmland.

I pushed myself hard as I navigated past wheat- and cornfields, pastureland, and the homesteads of farmers and ranchers that (to some degree) were our neighbors. It was all part of my teenaged strategy to increase my endurance and keep myself in top physical condition. I was relentless in my training.

If I wanted to play, I knew that I had to work harder than anyone else to make the team. My strategies paid off. As a sophomore in high school, I was awarded the most valuable player of the basketball state championship tournament. I also received all-conference recognition in volleyball and basketball for three consecutive years and an impressive collection of medals and ribbons in track and field.

Our coach believed in hardcore training as well. Before any game, there was practice. She believed that this is where a team won games. Our practice sessions were some of the most physically demanding and mentally brutal hours of our athletic careers.

We would rehearse offenses and defenses, fast breaks, full court presses, layups, jump shots, free throws, and everything in between, again and again, until it became automatic to us. Our coach's goal was to make our practice sessions so challenging that, on game day, we were a machine. Every time we stepped inside the lines that delineated the playing surface, we were calm, confident, and ready. Never arrogant, just ready.

I was born a loner, and I have always required an extraordinary amount of alone time. My lone wolf personality presented itself as extreme shyness until I was in fourth grade. Then, I discovered I was somewhat athletic. I started playing tetherball during recess in grade school and winning—a lot.

The more I played, the better I got. All of a sudden, I was kicking every kid's ass at tetherball. It didn't matter, boy or girl, I could beat them. When I wasn't smacking a ball around a pole, I would participate in jump roping. The kind where two kids stand about five yards apart and twirl two ropes in different directions and the jumper has to slip in at just the right moment to hop to the rhythm and speed of the spinning ropes.

As with most things, the more you rehearse an activity, the better you become. Every day when the recess bell rang, giving us a break from the classroom, I would go out onto the playground and hone my skills. I became less shy and more confident, and a pretty damn good jump-roper.

As I matured and started playing competitive sports in high school and college, I learned that being a lone wolf could be used to my advantage. I attribute the majority of my personal athletic success to this thing commonly known to most people as being in the "zone." I also refer to it as my beautiful place.

I had a peculiar way of getting into the "zone" before a game. It was my quiet, reliable place I would go before stepping onto a court or a track. I prepared for every game by going through this same routine. I didn't talk to my teammates—or anyone.

I didn't eat much on game days; I liked to play hungry. I would put my uniform on in a strict, ordered, and methodical way, wearing the same three pairs of tube socks for every game. By the end of the season, they were tattered and torn, but they served a vital purpose in my pregame psyche. While getting dressed, I would run through game plays in my head.

During warm-ups, I would start my journey into the "zone"—that quiet, precise, and alone place where I felt most comfortable and capable. Before the jump ball started each game, I would take my position on the court, bless myself with the sign of the cross, then go to that calm, worry-free, unemotional state. The only person I allowed myself to hear was my coach.

We drew large crowds to watch our games. Hundreds of fans would show up to support us. They were enthusiastic, loud, and ruthlessly haunting to our competitors. During our state championship games, there was not an empty seat in the house. People from all over the state of Colorado would travel to Denver to watch us play, adding to the roar of the crowd.

I never heard any of it. Only my coach. Not until I watched the game tapes would I hear the booming, forceful noise in the gym. This is the advantage of that beautiful place known as the "zone."

PAUSE AND REFLECT: FIND YOUR BEAUTIFUL PLACE

If you've ever been in the zone, you know what I'm talking about. If you've never been, I recommend the trip. It's a nonthinking, composed, sacred space. You feel safe and untouchable. Sheltered and in control, no one can get to you. I go there often and can access it quickly.

I remember watching a movie when I was a young girl. I don't remember the name of it or too much more about it other than what I am about to explain. There is a scene where several young men were standing on a football field preparing to be soldiers.

As part of their training, they were required to stand with their arms extended out to their sides, parallel to the ground, holding a bucket filled with concrete in each hand. All the while, a drill sergeant was walking amongst them, yelling for them not to give up. One by one, these men would drop the buckets to the ground as their arms gave way to the weight. But one guy remained.

He stood there all by himself with his eyes closed and sweat rolling down his face, holding those concrete-filled buckets. He never gave in to the weight or the screaming. He maintained this position until the drill sergeant instructed him to stop. When his superiors asked him how he was able to do this, he explained that he would picture in his mind the most beautiful place that he could imagine and he would focus on it so intently that he wasn't aware of anything else.

He didn't feel the pain in his body from holding the buckets. He didn't hear the bellowing of the drill sergeant. He had trained his mind to ignore those agitations and to concentrate purely on beauty. I will never forget this man or this movie. It had a huge influence on me. That day, I started practicing going to my "beautiful place."

I find this to be an effective tool that assists me in handling mind-over-matter situations in my life. Take a stab at employing this technique the next time you are faced with challenging circumstances. Discipline yourself to go to your beautiful place where nothing comes between you and the splendor of your mind.

Chapter Twelve

ENOUGH IS ENOUGH

"Courage—a perfect sensibility of the measure of danger, and a mental willingness to endure it."
— William T. Sherman

THE SUMMER BEFORE leaving the farm to go to college, I asked George if he would consider paying me for helping with the farming. He said no. Not long after his rejection was the last time I allowed George to verbally assault me. We were in one of our pastures, moving cows to an adjacent meadow.

The two were separated by a thin, round wire that stretched over hundreds of yards of land supported by fence posts. The barrier was effective at keeping our herd where we wanted them because it was an electric fence. Until they got used to it, many cows and calves would get shocked by unintentionally bumping into the wire or giving it a sniff out of curiosity.

George's strategy for getting the cows from one pasture to the other was to turn off the electric fence, prop the wire on top of thirty yards of fence posts, and drive the cattle underneath to the next pasture. In theory it made sense, but in reality, it was a dumbass idea. Why? Because the cows aren't stupid: they had come to understand that any encounter with an electric fence was painful.

George stayed in the pickup and told me to get out and start to push the cows toward the area where we had braced the wire on top of the posts, which would allow the cows to walk under the previously existing barrier to greener pastures. Well, guess what? Every time I would get the cows close to the so-called opening, they would scatter.

They had no way of knowing that 1) there was no juice running through the wire, and 2) they couldn't see that the fence had been raised, giving them clear passage. When the herd scattered, George would yell at me while he sat in the pickup, telling me how "fucking stupid" I was.

After the third failed attempt and after constant and unforgiving verbal abuse from George, something inside of me snapped. I had put up with a lifetime of his screaming insults and demeaning behavior, and I never once said anything or talked back to him. This time was different.

It was as if the giant within me burst out of its cage. I marched over to the passenger side of the pickup, got in, slammed the door shut, and said, "If you think you're so fucking smart, get off your fucking ass and move the fucking cows under the fucking fence by your fucking self." It was the first time I had ever said the "f" word out loud. But it wasn't the last.

I said it with such courage and conviction, George knew I was done putting up with his bullshit. We sat there in silence for a few minutes; then, he asked me how I thought we could move the cows. I told him to leave the electricity off for a few days with the wire propped on top of the fence posts, and eventually the cows would find their way to where we wanted them to go. Lo and behold, three days later, the entire herd was right where we wanted them.

As you might expect, my relationship with George was different after this. I felt more confident and realized that it was not okay with me to be on the receiving end of his outbursts. He backed off and gave me room to be myself. Our connection was cordial yet distant. I think that he understood that he had finally pushed me beyond what I was willing to tolerate and that his days of being a tyrant with me had come to an end.

Pause and Reflect: Bravery

Stopping to ponder this day in my life took some time and at least three, slow, contemplative swallows of some good red wine. The word that kept coming to me as I sat sunning myself nestled in a quiet and private outdoor hiding spot at my house was "bravery."

On that day in the pasture, I was brave enough to show up and say what needed to be said out loud. I could no longer suppress the discontent and fear that I held inside of me.

It was time to break free of the only rule of law I knew. I became an outlaw. The one thing that was fueling my courage was the fact that I was willing to put my vulnerability on the line. I had no control over the outcome, and I didn't care.

I have come to know that being loved and worthy is not a hustle. There is no performance required. The only thing needed is the guts to love yourself. It's always good to figure this out sooner rather than later. And, it's a damn shame that we are not taught this at the same time we are learning our A, B, C's.

So, my friend, be brave. If you find yourself in a situation or a relationship that you know is wrong, leave it. If someone is being disrespectful toward you either in conversation or action, speak up. If you need help with something, ask for it. Be brave enough to tell the truth and live the truth no matter what.

Chapter Thirteen

SHORTY

"A single conversation across the table with a wise person is worth a month's study of books."

— Chinese Proverb

IT WASN'T LONG after that I went to our neighbor's farm, Shorty, and asked if he needed help. He raised corn, wheat, and alfalfa. He said he could use a hand and wanted to know how much he would need to pay me. I left it up to him, depending on how hard of a worker he thought I was.

I went home and informed George I'd landed a paying job and wouldn't work for him anymore. As you can imagine, this wasn't the best news that George had ever received, but he knew. He knew that I had had an ah-ha moment that day in the pasture. And he knew there was nothing he could do about it.

The day after school was let out for the summer, I got in my Ford Mustang and drove the three miles to Shorty's farm to start my first paying job. I showed up every morning at 6 am, six days a week, ready to dive into the assigned task at hand.

I left every night at 6 pm, exhausted from an honest day's work. I drove tractors and trucks all over, doing everything from making sure the corn got irrigated on schedule, to moving irrigation pipe from one field to the next, to hauling alfalfa bales. I loved it. Shorty was a fascinating old guy.

He was a man of few words. A bachelor, who chain-smoked unfiltered Camel cigarettes and drank black coffee (that looked and smelled like sludge) all day long. His face was wrinkled and rugged from years of hard work. He was missing a number of teeth, and the neglected ones left were only seen on the rare occasions he would laugh.

We would drive to town each day to eat.

Taking a break for lunch was something foreign to me; all I knew was eating on the go. It took me a while to get used to these pauses in the day, as I felt like we had so much to do. But it was during these sit-downs that Shorty would tell me stories of his days as a rodeo cowboy. Rodeoing was his real passion, and he made a little money at it when he was a young man.

But his body took a beating, and finally, age and broken bones turned him back to farming. We worked hard that summer, and we accomplished a lot despite the daily lunch-hour respites. On my last day of work, Shorty pulled out his checkbook and paid me for my ten weeks of help.

I didn't know what to expect, but when I looked down, I saw the number: $1,620. It was the most money I had ever made in my entire life. Shorty told me I was the best farmhand he ever had, and the only girl. He said I proved how sturdy I was the day I ripped all the skin off the underside of my hands, pulling irrigation pipe apart with a rope, never stopping or complaining.

He thanked me for working fifteen-hour days during wheat harvest. He told me he hadn't laughed so much in a long time. He enjoyed our chats and liked that his crusty exterior didn't intimidate me. He asked me to stop by and see him when I came home from college.

I told him I would. As I drove out of his driveway that night, I looked in my rearview mirror and saw an old man—tears streaming down his cheeks—waving good-bye to a young girl with big dreams. He already missed me. What neither of us knew at the time is that I would be back the following summer. One last run at farming.

Chapter Fourteen

———— ❧ ————

THE END OF A FEW GOOD THINGS

"Hardships often prepare ordinary people for an extraordinary destiny."

— C. S. Lewis

I WENT HOME and packed my Mustang with clothes and a few other basics. The next day I was leaving for my first year of college. I attended Friends University in Wichita, Kansas. I chose Friends because I wanted to continue to play volleyball and basketball in college.

I didn't think I was decent enough to play for a team like Colorado State University or CU Boulder—those schools were big and intimidated me. I had been grappling with a bad knee during my last two years of high school, which is not attractive to college coaches and trainers.

As a side note, I recommend that you never choose second best. If I had it to do over again, I would have picked a school that would provide an excellent education as well as a challenging athletic opportunity. I would rather play second string for a great team than first string for a shitty team.

Friends was happy to have me, and they gave me an athletic scholarship, which helped to defray the costs of tuition. During my freshman year, I played in the starting line-up in both sports. The team's win-loss record was nothing to write home about, but I was acknowledged for my abilities through the collegiate athletic conference.

At the beginning of my second year at Friends, I sustained a knee injury that required surgery.

The team doctor who performed my surgery was a well-known, respected orthopedist who had taken care of the sports teams at Friends for years. He took his job seriously and cared deeply for the athletes. The day after my surgery, I sat on the exam table in his office.

With tears in his eyes, he told me my athletic career was over. My knee was a mess, and it would not withstand the rigors of being a competitor in the sports I loved. Hearing these words stopped time. I was in a moment where MY life stood still, while everyone else carried on.

I was on crutches for two months, shedding twenty-five pounds of muscle mass over three weeks, not knowing what to do with myself. I had a broken knee, and a broken heart. Not being able to participate in sports was a turning point in my life. I didn't realize how much of my identity was attached to being an athlete. I struggled.

I experienced emotions ranging from anger to self-pity. I realized my athletics had an endpoint. My injury meant my athletic scholarship went away. But—fortunately—I was a diligent student. My athletic scholarship turned into an academic one.

As essential as sports were to me, my main reason for going to college was a good education. My focus turned primarily to graduating with a Bachelor of Science degree in Business Administration. That summer, I went back home and resumed my employment with Shorty.

He was happy to have me, and I was glad to have a paying job. We picked up where we left off, working our asses off with our traditional, midday lunch break. Shorty recommended his storytelling, and I filled him in on my college tales. The days were long and dirty. I didn't see much of my parents or brothers.

My mom was off to the hospital each day, and my younger brother and George had their hands full with farming. By the end of the summer, I was tan from being outside every day. I was sturdy from moving irrigation pipe and tossing alfalfa bales around for ten weeks. And, my vocation as a farmer ended here.

The days of tractors and trucks and cattle and wheat harvests were over. I was leaving behind all that I knew and that which built my character. I was uncertain about what lay ahead, but it was undeniable that this part of my past would always hold a sacred and honored place in my heart.

After the dust settled from my knee surgery, I decided getting a part-time job would be a respectable way to spend the time I would otherwise be devoting to sports. Once I established my academic routine, I found a job working in a jewelry store. It provided me with much-needed income, and a means to transition out of a basketball uniform and into business attire.

It was an uncomfortable evolution because I started out with a minuscule wardrobe of appropriate clothing to wear as a jewelry salesperson; even my boss said I had to do better. Almost every dime I made went to putting ensembles on layaway that would be acceptable to wear to the first occupation I had outside of farming.

Imagine that: I was one hell of a tractor driver; I knew how to change the oil in farm equipment and build fences; I could haul bales and feed cattle; I could smack the shit out of volleyballs and score points on the basketball court—none of these activities happened while donning a skirt, dress, or pantsuit. Eventually, I assembled a few pieces of apparel that consisted of something other than cowboy boots, jeans, t-shirts, and athletic gear.

I learned a lot selling jewelry. From the time I was a young girl, diamonds had captured my attention. I remember walking through shopping malls with my mom, stopping at the windows of all of the jewelry shops to look at the bright, shiny diamonds. Rubies and sapphires were pretty, but I was always a diamond girl. During slow times, I tried on every single diamond ring in the store.

I felt like it was an excellent sales strategy because I knew the inventory well and I could point out all of the best qualities and details of engagement rings, wedding bands, and cocktail rings. I would study the four "C's" of diamonds—Cut, Color, Clarity, and Carat size—so that I could educate the customers about the importance of each and why it contributed to the value of the rings they bought.

I also began to realize the value of putting smiles on customers' faces and the significance of serving others. I learned about tracking sales, reporting data to the corporate office, doing bank deposits, ordering inventory, and all back-office details essential to the daily operation of the store. This little job was my first taste of the business world.

PAUSE AND REFLECT: A FORK IN THE ROAD

My knee injury and the transitions that came with it was the first time that I realized that life events like this create a fork in the road. We get to choose what path we are going to take as we go forward. Up until this point, I hadn't spent much time thinking specifically about what I wanted to do with my life.

I knew that studying business was a pragmatic choice and a stable foundation on which to build a reasonable future. I had visions of having my own company one day, and I knew for sure that I did not want to be poor. As I look back on this time in my life, I was making it up as I went. I had no plan. I had no guidance. I had no idea.

What I knew for sure was that I had to keep moving forward; stepping into the days ahead with naiveté was part of the process of becoming. It is times like this when we discover, develop, and deepen who we are; it gives us the chance to embrace the impermanence of our identity because it can and will change. It provides us with the occasion to adjust and adapt and grow. It is an invitation to give ourselves some grace. Life is dynamic, and our biggest challenge and opportunities lie in finding harmony in the movement and perceived chaos that comes our way.

What have been some of the forks in the road that you have encountered in your life's journey? Would you handle them the same way today as you did then? What did you learn about yourself and others in these situations that provide you with valuable tools as you evolve in your life?

It is what we gain from these occurrences that becomes the wind beneath our wings as we walk through each day. The remarkable thing about life is that we get to change and adapt and grow. And, it is often the most perplexing, painful, and confusing events that render the ultimate prospects for advancement.

Chapter Fifteen

LIFE GOES ON

"And suddenly you know ... It's time to start something new and trust the magic of beginnings."

— Eckhart Tolle

IMMEDIATELY AFTER GRADUATING from Friends University, I accepted a position with Fourth National Bank, the largest banking institution in the state of Kansas. I was part of a six-month training program that allowed us to spend time in each area of the bank before picking a department in which to work.

I ended up in the marketing department as a portfolio manager for commercial accounts. I enjoyed it because I could go into the community and meet the owners and leaders of the local companies. I'd spend time with them, learning about their businesses, how they started them, what their future strategies were, and how the bank could assist them in reaching their goals.

These people were generous with their time, and many of them helped to spark the entrepreneurial fire in me. I began to network myself, getting involved in the local Chamber of Commerce and other organizations. I loved the professional life and all that came with it. Except the pay.

It was about this time I met a young man who worked at the Residence Inn Company. It was relatively new and founded by a local businessman, Jack DeBoer. It was the first extended-stay hotel brand in the United States and the leading player in launching the suite concept in a hotel.

I was offered a job at twice the pay I was making at the bank, so, hello? I made the move. I went to Denver for my sales training, then moved to Sunnyvale, California, to assist in building the occupancy rate in the middle of the booming Silicon Valley. The adjustment was challenging for me because I didn't know many people, and the extended-stay hotel business was a far cry from banking.

It was a rocky start once I got to Sunnyvale. The properties were struggling to build occupancy. The sales staff had recently had some turnover, so there was no leadership or direction. But there was plenty of room in the hotel, and I was young, flexible, and uncertain about my next living arrangement. So, I lived on the property.

My residency provided me a fantastic opportunity to learn the ins and outs of the operations of the hotel while helping to cover my cost of living. I picked up on the uniqueness of the property versus other hotels in the market. The General Manager and National Director of Sales sat down with me and, together, we developed a plan to reach sales and revenue targets.

After six months of focus and diligence, our dedicated team had not only met our goals—we had surpassed them. Hard work always pays off. I became the Director of Sales and held that position until I was asked to move back to the corporate headquarters in Wichita to be part of the franchise development team.

My time living on a property and learning the sales tactics and other characteristics that made a Residence Inn successful helped me with my new task. I was assigned the Northeastern United States as my territory. For the next year, I spent most of my time traveling throughout New York, Pennsylvania, and New England searching for land sites and potential franchisees to expand the Residence Inn brand.

I spent so much time on airplanes, I got to know the flight attendant crews to the point we became friends. I knew every exit off the I-95 and I-84 freeways, all the way between Maine, New York, and Pennsylvania. I knew the best land brokers in every real-estate market, and forged relationships with them all.

I met with bankers and commercial real-estate developers to get leads as to who might be a possible franchisee. I learned the lay of the land and mapped out what companies resided in the area. I perused local business rags daily to understand the business environment and economic climate in each market.

I met my fair share of shady landowners and their representatives, a handful of them with mafia connections. I set up as many meetings as possible, most of them with men, on my own, and at only twenty-three years old. The male-dominated environment I operated in was never a challenge for me. After all, I had been surrounded by guys my entire life.

PAUSE AND REFLECT: #BeIn

It doesn't matter if you are a woman or a man reading this. I am not seeking agreement, and I am open to disagreement. It is my belief that there is plenty of room for all of us to make a contribution in the world without stepping on each other's toes or getting in each other's way.

I have spent my entire working life in industries that would likely be considered "male-dominated." After all, I started out as a farmer and then went into banking. Banking turned into real-estate development and after that, health care and consumer products. In every single one of these situations, there have been more men involved than women.

I have never viewed this as a disadvantage or a pitfall or a problem. Quite the contrary. I have always considered being a woman in each of these endeavors to be an advantage, a benefit, and an opportunity. I am not a "lean in" fan. Instead, I encourage women and men to "be in." Be yourself; that's all. If you bring your best self, your true self, to your job, your work environment, your vocation, your business, and your industry, everyone wins.

The Japanese have a term called *ikigai*. Wikipedia describes the concept as follows:

Ikigai (生き甲斐, pronounced [ikigai]) is a Japanese concept that means 'a reason for being.' The word 'ikigai' is usually used to indicate the source of value in one's life or the things that make one's life worthwhile. The word translated into English roughly means 'thing that you live for' or 'the reason for which you wake up in the morning.'

Each individual's ikigai is personal to them and specific to their lives, values, and beliefs. It reflects the inner self of an individual and expresses that faithfully, while simultaneously creating a mental state in which the individual feels at ease. Activities that allow one to feel ikigai are never forced on an individual; they are often spontaneous, and always undertaken willingly, giving the individual satisfaction and a sense of meaning to life.

I urge you to find clarity for your "reason for being." If you are waking up each morning focused on the "thing that you live for," there will be no time or space for anger. You will not look for people or things that may offend you. Instead, you will be in a state of ease regardless of the vigor of your activities and involvements.

Know this: there is greatness in you. What you have to offer the world is remarkable. When your heart speaks, listen to it. Honor it. Allow yourself to be all that you are meant to become. And, hold space for others to do the same. Remember, there is room for all of us.

A CHANGE OF COURSE

Just when I was hitting full stride and contributing to the growth of the franchise side of the business, Marriott Corporation bought Residence Inn. The purchase was a feather in the cap for Jack and many of his executive team. It was also a well-deserved achievement for him.

It was only twelve years earlier that he'd run into deep financial trouble as the apartment building business he was involved in went upside down. After the Marriott deal, Jack went on to be very successful as the founder or cofounder of extended-stay hotels and short-term apartment concepts.

Jack is the author of the book *Risk Only Money*. In the book, he shares all the things that he learned the hard way. DeBoer is a straight shooter and tells his story with integrity and transparency. Wherever you are in your life's journey, you will find the sage advice of DeBoer to be a sincere invitation to live a life of significance.

It took several weeks for the dust to settle after Marriott purchased the company. Marriott kept the bulk of the Residence Inn employees in place, including me. However, their future development strategy for the brand was for the majority of the hotels to be corporate-owned, eliminating the need for franchise development personnel.

After a good deal of discussion and just as much concern about my ability to handle a corporate real-estate position, I convinced the department head that I had what it would take to meet his expectations. So, at twenty-five years old, I relocated to Boston, Massachusetts, representing Marriott Corporation in purchasing land for up to one million dollars per acre and building hotels at the cost of $7 to $15 million apiece—and they were concerned about my capability? Come on.

I joined two terrific guys who handled two other hotel brands under the Marriott umbrella. Since I had spent most of the previous year in the territory sniffing out franchise opportunities, I was ready to hit the ground running. For the next two and a half years—with the assistance of a dedicated team of attorneys, civil engineers, land brokers, and corporate support folks—we built five hotels, with five more in the pipeline.

I learned a ton, I met a lot of amazing people, and I accomplished some self-goals in the process. However, I felt something was missing. As much as I valued and appreciated the work I was doing, I felt I was destined for something else. Something bigger, I guess. So, I did what I always did. I looked to my North Star to help me determine my next move. She never led me wrong. Somehow, we decided ... MBA.

Chapter Sixteen

———— ∾ ————

HARVARD OR BUST

"I quite possibly could have been one of HBS's greatest experiments."
— Annie M. Fonte

I RESEARCHED WHAT I thought were the top five business schools in the country: Harvard, Stanford, Wharton, Northwestern, and the University of Chicago. My examination was scant, at best. I knew next to nothing about any of them, except they had all been around awhile, and each had a high-ranking reputation.

It is reasonable to think that it would have made sense to apply to each of these institutions of higher learning. But no, not me. I wanted to go to what I considered the best school in the world. I narrowed it down to Harvard Business School. As I look back now, I had no idea what I was doing or what I was getting myself into, let alone giving any thought to how I was going to pay for this brainstorm. At the time, I could have been the poster child for "ignorance is bliss."

Harvard's campus was twelve miles from my house. I didn't even have to call or write to have an application sent to me; I just swung by to pick one up. Surely, this whole process was going to be a breeze. In reality, every step of the way was like walking uphill in lead-lined boots.

When I went to pick up the application, it took me thirty minutes to find parking. The paperwork required completing seventeen essay questions, none of which were uncomplicated, and all of which were thought-provoking and time-consuming. I took a question with me each day to work, so when I was driving, which I did a lot of, I could think about how I was going to answer it. When I got home, I would write out my answer, then move on to the next query.

It turned out Harvard Business School had four separate application deadlines, so I figured the earlier I entered in my application, the better chance I had (which—let's be honest—was a snowball's chance in hell). But maybe if I busted my ass to get it done by the first deadline … maybe?

It took me four months to get my application deemed fit for submission. I contacted the school and asked where I could hand-deliver what I considered to be a brilliantly completed pile of paperwork that would undoubtedly gain me my acceptance to Harvard Business School.

Once again—after at least thirty minutes of driving around to find a parking spot—I proudly walked into the Admissions Office to hand over my self-proclaimed masterpiece. As I walked through the doors, I encountered a portly man with dubious attention to personal hygiene sitting behind a desk, surrounded by piles of what turned out to be other people's so-called masterpieces.

Yep, this guy was encircled with thousands of applications from individuals all over the world who wanted a seat at Harvard. Even though I was stunned to see this pile of massive evidence that Harvard was a much-sought-after MBA program, I proudly handed my envelope to the man at the desk.

Without looking at me, he gave a slight grunt of acknowledgment, snatched my packet away from me, and casually tossed it into the pile of other applications behind him. I stood in disbelief, witnessing an act of pure disdain from a man who looked like his heart would attack him at any moment.

He did not give one shit about the thousands of wannabe MBAs who were competing for a spot at one of the most prestigious business schools in the world. He was more intent on sucking the sugary soda from the straw of his Super Big Gulp that was sitting in a pool of its own sweat on his desk.

I walked out of the building that day thinking it would be the last time I would see the storied walls of this historic university. It was time to get back to work. I had learned a lot, chasing the absurd idea of thinking I could go to a school of such high esteem. I mean, c'mon. I was just a farm girl from the middle of nowhere who used to sit on my tractor, fantasizing about such grandeur.

It would be a miracle if anyone found my application, let alone read it. And, either way, it would be three or four months before I would be informed of a likely rejection or a highly improbable acceptance to pursue a master's degree in business. So, I went back to doing what I knew—the hotel business.

Then the day came. Four uncertain months after I surrendered my application to the surly dude in the Admissions Office, I got an answer. I reached into my mailbox, and an envelope with a return address of "Harvard Business School" was staring me in the face. My first thought was, *This envelope is light. It doesn't take a lot of words to tell someone they've been denied acceptance to one of the most coveted MBA programs in the world.*

I walked back and forth, trying to decide what to do. This was my future, and the chances were as slim as the envelope. Screw it. I grabbed a sharp knife—a very sharp knife—slid the blade gently under the flap, and rescued that single piece of paper from its confines. One deep breath later, I unfolded a typewritten letter. My eyes locked on the first word I saw: "*Congratulations.*"

Un-flippin' believable. Someone had actually found my master-piece and, for whatever reason, decided to give me a chance. They said yes, the universe said yes, and I said yes! At least for a minute. Then the second thoughts started rolling in. All of a sudden, I was conflicted.

Do I give up a job that pays six figures in exchange for an advanced education that costs six figures? Do I leave everything I know for something completely unknown? Do I concede the next two years of my life to change the trajectory of the rest of my life? Do I have any idea what I am doing? No, No, No, and No.

I went for a walk to collect myself, and it came to me. One day, when you are on your deathbed, will you regret not going to Harvard? The answer was a short, sweet, and definitive YES. I don't know about you, but it is times like this that a gal wants to call people and tell them the news.

I was so excited and proud and nervous and scared. I just had to tell someone. I phoned a handful of friends, my brother, and my mom to reveal my acceptance. They were all so happy for me. They were just as giddy as I was. And then, I called George. I told him that I had been accepted to Harvard Business School. The first words out of his mouth were, "Well, who the fuck is going to pay for that?"

My heart sank like a runaway elevator plummeting to the maximum depth of despair in less than a moment. His reaction left me breathless and speechless for a handful of seconds, and then I collected myself. I assured George that I would somehow figure out how to fund this chance of a lifetime that he considered to be a high-priced boondoggle.

Ugh. When would I ever learn that this guy was never going to be the proud and encouraging dad that I had hoped that he would be? Never, ever.

Pause and Reflect: You Miss Every Single Shot You Don't Take

Listen to me. If you really want to do something, figure out how to get it done. You might have experienced some "Harvard or Bust" moments in your life. Heck, you might be squarely in the middle of a similar situation as you read these words. I know that it is frightening. And believe me, I would be doing you a disservice if I didn't tell you that there are going to be jolts along the way.

There will be unexpected wallops that send your heart and your hopes nose-diving to uneasy depths of anguish. People will tell you that you are zany to have such aspirations. Do it anyway. Once you decide, the fear dissipates. Let's be honest: getting into Harvard Business School was a long shot for me. Even so, I was resolved to give it my best shot because you never know.

Here is the other thing to keep in mind: Notice I didn't just up and quit my job, leaving me no safety net if Harvard said no. You have to think these things through. If you have what you think is a trillion-dollar idea, do the research and test the waters as a side hustle before you pull the trigger.

If you want to write a book, get up an hour earlier each day and write. Write during your lunch break. Write for one hour before you hit the hay each night. Eventually, those focused hours of authorship turn into your book.

If you are looking for a raise at work, sit down with your boss and ask them how you could add more value to the organization. Better yet, tell them how you think you can help decrease expenses and increase revenues. Become so beneficial to the company that they can't afford to lose you.

And finally, you probably will never feel like you are absolutely ready to take a shot. This is what keeps most people from stepping into their greatness. *The lack of certainty or the fear of failure are potent culprits of possibility and potential.* Don't be the guy or gal who goes to your grave with a book or an invention or a screenplay or a cure locked inside of you. Take the shot.

Chapter Seventeen

IGNORANCE IS NOT BLISS

"Ignorance is not bliss, it is oblivion."

— Philip Wylie

So, THAT WAS it. I was going to accept the invitation to attend Harvard Business School in the fall. I had a few months to tie up some loose ends before starting an experience for which I was utterly unprepared. I notified Marriott that I would be leaving at the end of the summer, giving them plenty of time to fill my position.

I secured on-campus housing and lined up student loans (which scared the shit out of me). I started to read through the enormous piles of "summer reading" found in my mailbox that I had to absorb before school started in the fall. I went to a Q&A session created and run by the soon-to-be second-year students and alumni who lived locally.

One of my fellow new students asked the experienced ones to describe the first year at HBS. There were many versions of the same answer, which was, basically, "It's a two-year underwater swim." It turns out I was clueless about what I was getting myself into, which was two of the most ruthless years of my life—at least up to this point.

Before applying to—and later attending—HBS, I knew two things. One, it was a distinguished school. And two, I wanted to go there. Here's what I didn't realize (get comfortable, the list is long):

1. The year I was accepted, less than 11% of the applicants got awarded a seat in the class. 28% were women, 33% were international students.
2. Grades are based 50% on class participation, 50% on one or two written exams in each course.
3. Many of my classmates had a parent or relative who had attended HBS.
4. Several of my classmates' parents were big donors to HBS.
5. Many of my classmates had been groomed to go to HBS their whole lives; some had attended boarding schools and private schools from a very young age.
6. Some of my classmates had well-known or famous parents.
7. Parents or employers paid for the MBA education of at least 50% of my classmates.
8. School transcripts, extracurricular activities, awards, post-MBA career goals, test scores, and letters of recommendation weigh heavily on your likelihood of admittance.
9. There were three ways to get out of HBS: you could graduate, you could quit, or you could flunk out. Up to 10% of the class would "hit the screen" and potentially be asked to leave by the academic performance committee.
10. The grading system consisted of a 1, 2, 3, or 4. A 1 is given to the top 15–20% of the students in each required class; a 2 is given to the next 70–75% of the students, a 3 is given to the lowest-performing students, and a 4, which is rarely given, goes to anyone failing the curriculum.
11. The workload is humanly impossible to complete each evening as one prepares for the following day's class sessions.

12. The classroom environment is mercilessly competitive.
13. Most of my classmates came from engineering, consulting, or investment banking backgrounds.
14. Alumni include a past President of the United States and those in 20% of the top three jobs at Fortune 500 companies.
15. Extraordinary guest speakers include—to name a few—Bill Gates, Sir Richard Branson, the Ferragamo family, Ben and Jerry, and John Sculley.
16. When I stepped onto campus, I knew no one among the student body or faculty.
17. The entire HBS curriculum is case studies based on real-world business situations.
18. The first year is spent in a U-shaped, five-tiered classroom. The bottom tier is called the Worm Deck; the top tier is called the Sky Deck. The room houses eighty to ninety students known as your section mates. (I was in Section H.)
19. HBS is known as the West Point of capitalism.
20. It is said to accept a high number of aggressively materialistic, self-centered students.
21. It seemed like every single person in my class was smarter and more prepared to be at HBS than me.

It was daunting to be part of such a potent pedigree of future leaders. From the very first day of class, I never felt like I fit in with this elite group of young men and women who were determined to make a name for themselves in the business world. After all, these folks had put a lot of time and effort into being part of the ivy-covered gateway to the upper stratum of corporations all over the planet.

I remember sitting in class as the people who would make up Section H entered the room and selected a seat that would be theirs for the rest of the year. I quietly settled into my Sky Deck chair and noticed that almost everyone in the room seemed to know each other.

I leaned over to one of my section-mates and asked if I had missed an orientation gathering, as everyone seemed to be friends. She said no, that her dad had gone to HBS with that one's dad, and their dads were both top executives at a Fortune 100 company, then proceeded to point out all the heavy-hitters with major Harvard connections.

For about the third time in this process, I felt like I'd been sucker-punched. At that moment, I realized I was starting out way behind the eight ball. During the first few weeks of the program, we were encouraged to form study groups. This meant finding four or five other students to meet with every night to review and discuss the following day's cases.

One way to find your clan was to examine the resume book containing the curriculum vitae of each of your classmates. After reading through a couple of dozen randomly picked resumes, I was confident I did not belong at HBS, and I'd been chosen as part of a cruel experiment to see how long a green-behind-the-ears dirt farmer could last in a program designed for the best of the best.

I bounced around to two or three groups until I settled in with one of my female section-mates and two men from another section. We would meet each night at 10:30 pm to begin our analysis of the following day's cases. The agreement was to have already read the cases and have started—if not completed—our individual evaluation of each.

Most nights we would wrap things up around 12:30 am, in some instances, going even longer. I would then go back to my dorm room and spend more time preparing, because the last thing I wanted to experience was to be called on by a professor to open a case when I wasn't geared up to do so.

Sleep was a much-sought-after commodity that escaped my grasp nineteen to twenty hours a day. I learned to survive on those delicious three to four hours of slumber per night. I studied seven days a week. I rarely socialized outside the classroom, not because I didn't want to, but because I didn't feel like I could spare the time.

Although I didn't feel like I belonged, I wanted to be at Harvard, and it was my desire to graduate with an MBA. I was determined to learn as much as I could. After all, I was paying for a very costly education that, with opportunity cost added in, came to well over a quarter of a million dollars.

Even though I didn't come from a legacy family and was far from being noble in any way, shape, or form, I was proud to be at this school—and I was going to make damn sure I graduated from it.

Pause and Reflect: No Matter What

We all want to feel like we matter. Heck, love and belonging are smack dab in the middle of Maslow's hierarchy of human needs. But sometimes I think we try too hard to fit in, to be loved, to belong. So much so that we sacrifice ourselves to please others. Let's face it: I didn't fit into the elite profile of a Harvard Business School student.

There was no denying it, so acceptance was the most sensible way through it. It was uncomfortable to not resemble an ideal of conformity. This was when I reminded myself to live my own truth. I didn't have anything to prove. For me, being at Harvard was not about being comfortable; it was about completing a milestone in my life that I was committed to, no matter what.

I came to know within myself that I didn't fit in with the Harvard bunch, but I damn well belonged there. I wasn't born to fit in or to walk with the crowd. Over time, I reached the liberating conclusion that I would rather sit in a room among the herd in the solace of being myself than attempting to fit in feeling hollowed out on the inside.

Life is so much easier when we step fully into our true essence. Trust me on this; don't wear a mask or a cloak or a costume. Have the courage to un-become all that you are not so that you can unapologetically become all that you are. I don't know about you, but I believe in something bigger than myself; for me, it's God.

For you, it might be the Universe or Source or Goddess or Supreme Being; it doesn't matter. My point is that God created me in His image. He made me stand out from anyone else. He crafted me as a one and only. And whoever or whatever you believe in, did the same for you.

God does not make junk—He crafts masterpieces and you are one of them. Not fully embracing who you are and your uniqueness is like telling God that He didn't do a good enough job when He built you. Stop the madness. The concept of fitting in is bullshit. The notion of being yourself is priceless. Start right now. Take full ownership of your life, and be you.

Chapter Eighteen

———— ❧ ————

TUSSLE FOR A TASSEL

"Each new epoch in life seems an encounter. There is a tussle and a cloud of dust, and we come out of it triumphant or crest-fallen, according as we have borne ourselves."
— Henry Wadsworth Longfellow

IT WAS NOT uncommon for my classmates' parents to visit during the year and attend a class or two. They were always impeccably dressed, the moms decked out in the most exquisite jewelry. My peers would proudly introduce them, often stating they'd come to see what they were spending their money on, which would garner a chuckle from the professors and some students.

I often envied the kids whose moms and dads would drop in to check on them. I thought how incredible it must be to be free of the financial burden this advanced degree brought with it. And I was most certainly open to their parents buying me a sandwich if they had a few extra dollars lying around.

I'd used up all of my savings to help pay for tuition and maxed out what I was eligible for in student loans. The workload of the program prohibited me from acquiring a part-time job, so I lacked in the money department. I couldn't afford to eat three meals a day, so I would buy Bazooka bubble gum for a penny a piece.

I would go for a long walk almost every day after class to get some fresh air and clear my head before starting in on casework for the next day. More often than not, I would find spare change in my travels, which helped defray the cost of gum. Chewing the gum enabled me to keep my hunger at bay, and the Bazooka Joe comic strips were generally good for a half-hearted laugh.

That said, I was fortunate to have good friends who lived in Charlestown, which was about a three-mile walk from campus. On most Friday nights they would invite me for a home-cooked meal and send me home with any leftovers. I would walk there, even in a blizzard, stopping at a shopping mall along the way to study and make it to their house before it got dark.

We would chat about the week, have a nice meal, then they'd drive me back to my dorm. They were a lifeline to me; I'm not sure what I would have done without them. I kept my financial situation to myself; even my friends who fed me every week didn't know the struggle I was facing. Being in this vulnerable condition brought with it feelings of shame.

I didn't compare myself to my classmates or have any anger towards them about their financial condition versus mine, but I was embarrassed I couldn't do better for myself. The majority of their worlds were so vastly different from mine, but this actually made me appreciate my humble beginnings and unsophisticated existence that much more.

My childhood taught me not to focus on what I didn't have, but to value what I did. This time at HBS allowed me to look for the hope beneath the hopelessness, and to pierce the noise of the world to hear the unspoken messages of encouragement. And, most importantly, to stay true to me.

I kept my ass planted firmly in the saddle. There was nothing to be gained from putting on a mask and endeavoring to fit in because I didn't really fit in at all. The only thing most of my classmates and I had in common was the fact that we showed up in the same buildings each day, yearning that in a few months' time we would walk across a stage wearing a costume called a cap and gown and be handed a piece of paper called a diploma.

I made a handful of friends during my two-year tenure at HBS, only a few of whom I've stayed in touch with over the years. I didn't take full advantage of the networking opportunities offered by attending a school renowned for its worldwide grid of connections, but I did absorb priceless bits of wisdom that have served me well throughout my life.

HBS taught me a distinctive way of thinking and making decisions. I learned how to get to the nuts and bolts of situations quickly and efficiently. I was uncomfortable every single day at Harvard. The discomfort gave me the gift of getting comfortable with uneasiness.

I learned how to figure out the limiting step in any process and determine the best way to get it handled. I came to understand that the business environment can be unforgiving and malicious, just like HBS. And—most importantly—I learned that anything is possible if you are willing for it to be.

Pause and Reflect: You Get to Decide

My two years at Harvard Business School were a tussle. Nothing about it was easy. And it was certainly not something people from Wray, Colorado, did. So far, I'm the only one from that tiny little farming community in the middle of nowhere who has attempted and succeeded in swimming in the shark-infested waters of Harvard Business School.

Entire books have been written about the experience, each telling the story from the author's perspective. I, too, could transcribe many pages, detailing that mentally excruciating period of my life, but

I think you get the idea. Truth be told, it really is a privilege and luxury to have spent time on the battlefield of the Ivy League.

The point is that you can accomplish anything if you are willing to make the sacrifices necessary to get it done. Quitting or making excuses is a sure sign that the task at hand just isn't important enough to you. The good news is, YOU get to decide.

Just because it has never been done doesn't mean that it can't happen.

If I would have fixated on all of the explanations of why attending Harvard was unachievable, I would have not ever ended up there. It is no different than Colonel Sanders who, at age sixty-two with a $105 Social Security check in hand, set out to propose his chicken recipe to restaurants and was turned down by 1,009 people.

They told him he was crazy. The rejections led to Kentucky Fried Chicken. Thomas Edison failed over 10,000 times before he successfully invented a workable commercial lightbulb. He never considered himself a failure. He chalked it up to discovering over 9,999 ways that an electric lightbulb wouldn't work.

And then there is J. K. Rowling, the divorced, jobless, penniless single parent who wrote the Harry Potter books while sitting in coffee shops. She was rebuffed seventeen times by publishers before a small publishing house in the U.K. gave her a trivial advance and printed 1,000 copies of her book. Today, Rowling has sold more than 400 million copies of her books.

There are thousands of versions of these same stories throughout history. The one thing these folks all have in common is they never gave up. They concentrated on what was possible and they believed in themselves. It didn't matter what other people told them.

It didn't matter that the deck was stacked against them; they refused to quit. As Saint Francis of Assisi once said, "Start by doing what is necessary; then do what is possible; and suddenly you are doing the impossible."

Meeting Robert

In between my first and second year at Harvard, I traveled to San Diego, California, for a summer job with TheraTx—a start-up company founded by three friends: Robert, Bret, and Kip.

TheraTx provided multidisciplinary rehabilitation services in skilled nursing facilities throughout the United States. Robert was an HBS graduate and the president of the company. I did a lot of number-crunching for Robert as he prepared to meet with venture capital investors to raise the third-and-final round of funding for the business.

I enjoyed being part of a tiny little enterprise, with only nine employees at the time, including the founders. We worked long and hard and had a lot of fun. Nine weeks after arriving, I drove back to Boston to begin my second year of business school. Just like the first year, it was a grind, but at least I knew what to expect.

HBS graduates are some of the most sought-after pieces of flesh for companies that make up the "who's who" of global business. The number of organizations showing up on campus each year, hoping to add an HBS grad to their payroll, is two to four times the number of students seeking employment. The school's recruiting policies and guidelines make *War and Peace* look like a pamphlet.

The content was no doubt hammered out by a bevy of attorneys who left no stone unturned. Being witness to recruiting week was yet another notch in my belt of "I do not fit in." I remember looking out of my dorm room window, watching a sea of hundreds of my peers—both men and women—dressed in dark suits and starched white shirts, swimming into the waters churned by the most powerful corporate entities in existence.

I thought how crazy this all was: students scurrying around, putting their best selves forward, as they lined up to sell their souls to corporate titans of rapacious repute. Although I had no intentions of going into consulting, investment banking, or manufacturing, I thought I should at least go to a couple of interviews. As it turned out, the interviewers were some of the most uptight people I had ever met.

And remember—I was surrounded by hundreds of anxious people every day. While I was determined to find a start-up company or an entrepreneurial environment to be in, my classmates were accepting six-figure offers with handsome sign-on bonuses, mouthwatering perks, and benefits packages.

I had stayed in contact with Robert since completing my summer job with his company a few months earlier. We were having a phone conversation one day, and he asked if I'd like to come back to work with him. He said it wouldn't be the best offer, but the best opportunity.

He wanted me to join his small team and assist him in growing his company, with the goal of taking it public within three years. I said yes and was excited to get back to San Diego to reconvene with my colleagues at TheraTx. But first, I needed to graduate from Harvard.

I don't remember a lot about graduation, except that my brother Dan told me, no matter what, he would be there. Although I don't think he was in the financial position to travel from Colorado to Boston for the event, he kept his promise. He showed up with my older brother and George in tow. Talk about fish out of water.

Wearing his best shirt and blue jeans, Dan congratulated every man, woman, or child that he met whether they were graduating from Harvard or not. His logic was, if you were on campus that day, you must have done something right, so it was hats off to all. He was genuinely happy for every single person there.

My mom also came. She and George had been divorced for a handful of years by then, but everyone put their best foot forward, and by the end of it, I had a diploma from Harvard Business School.

Chapter Nineteen

———∾∾———

ROBERT

"Grief is like the ocean; it comes in waves, ebbing and flowing. Sometimes the water is calm, and sometimes it is overwhelming. All we can do is learn to swim."

— Vicki Harrison

AFTER GRADUATION, I packed up my stuff and made my way to California. I got settled in and was entirely focused on my role at TheraTx. As with most small companies, the workload was endless. The days started early and the nights ended late. But I was learning a lot, and Robert was generous with his time and wisdom as he led his growing enterprise.

Then, three months into my post-graduate journey, I was thrown a life-changing curveball. Robert started to experience severe itching all over his body, and his skin had taken on a jaundiced appearance. He thought it was an allergy of some sort and went to his doctor to find some relief.

After seeing a couple of skin specialists and going through a battery of tests, he had a diagnosis. With a tear in his eye, Robert walked into my office and told me he'd been handed a death sentence. He had a rare and aggressive form of cancer called cholangiocarcinoma. The chances of survival: four percent. How could this be?

He was a thirty-nine-year-old man with a beautiful wife, three- and five-year-old daughters, a baby on the way, and a fifteen-year-old daughter from a previous marriage. It did not make any sense to me. Navigating the next nine months was challenging, inspiring, and ultimately, heartbreaking.

Within weeks of his diagnosis, Robert had liver resection surgery followed by aggressive chemotherapy, all in the attempt to rid his body of this belligerent disease. Soon after surgery, he was feeling better and attended the birth of his fourth daughter, Diana Hope. Diana was a family name, and Robert chose Hope as her middle name for obvious reasons.

Robert had a way with people. He was a charismatic leader who expressed his appreciation for everyone in his company. He was a devoted husband and a hands-on dad. He was also a loyal and caring friend. Over the next several months he was in and out of the hospital frequently, as the side effects of chemo raised their ugly head.

My apartment was only minutes from the hospital, so I would visit almost daily during the times he was hospitalized. Some nights he would call to ask if I could come to talk with him or read to him. His home was a forty-five-minute drive from the hospital, and his wife had her hands full with three young children.

Once he was home, I would sit with him at their house if his wife needed to run errands. I would sneak him his favorite Mexican food any time he had a craving. I would tell him what was going on at the office in his absence. In turn, he would share his thoughts.

He told me he was afraid that he might die soon. He asked me to help write down things that he wanted to get in place for his daughters so they would have memories of him throughout their lives. He asked that I stay with the company long enough to assist with the transition of a new president and a corporate headquarters' move to Atlanta.

And, finally, he asked if I would be a pallbearer at his funeral. How could such a high honor feel so shitty? Nine months after Robert learned he had cancer, death picked his number. I stood next to his casket with five men, all of us wearing dark suits and white gloves.

I reached for a handle, knowing it would be my final grasp before saying good-bye to a magnificent man who had come to mean so much to me. That day, I lost a friend and a mentor. I felt adrift. I felt like I had gone through hell, swallowed by heartache. It is rare to cross paths with an individual who leaves such an indelible mark on our lives. Robert was one of those people.

He taught me the importance of leading from behind to ensure that everyone in front was safe and on course. He showed me that being an entrepreneur was extremely risky, but the rewards—when they came—could be abundant. He instilled in me the significance of being prepared, regardless of the situation.

He coached me on the possible pitfalls of being a woman in a male-dominated business climate. He showed me that everything is figure-out-able. And he insisted on having fun, no matter how taxing the state of affairs. This man will always hold a sacred part of my heart. And, he was right: he did give me my best opportunity.

TheraTx was not the same without Robert at the helm. I didn't much care for the new president. I felt like he lacked authenticity, and he never gained my trust, but I kept my promise to Robert and made sure I executed on his requests before deciding to leave the company.

Pause and Reflect: Loss

When someone drives away without us and with no intention of coming back, it sucks. They pack up and leave and just like that, we will never see them again—at least in the flesh-and-bone human form. However, it seems to me that when we are ready to leave this experience of our life and move on, there is no holding us back. It is those of us who are left behind that suffer. It is part of the human condition.

We miss the person who went. Our heart aches for their physical presence all the while missing the signs of them everywhere. We are pissed at whatever vehicle that they chose to drive off in—cancer, heart attack, an accident—and we wonder if there was anything more we could have done to convince them to stay around a bit longer.

It is hard to forget those who gave us so much to remember. But those who choose death are ready for the next great adventure. It is painful to let go of someone you treasure and love. However, I have come to know that when we lose someone or something, we also gain so much.

May the memories of the one you lost bring you laughter in your quiet moments. May their courage and certainty at the end of their life bring you the same certainty and courage in your own life. And, may their absence bring you more presence as you traverse through this precious thing called life.

There is a quote by Teal Swan that goes like this: "A thousand times we die in one life. We crumble, break, and tear apart until the layers of illusion are burned away and all that is left, is the truth of who and what we really are." Let the gift of a loved one's death be that you are closer to the truth.

After Robert's death, a friend sent me this poem by Mary Elizabeth Frye:

> *Do not stand at my grave and weep*
> *I am not there. I do not sleep.*
> *I am a thousand winds that blow.*
> *I am the diamond glints on snow.*
> *I am the sunlight on ripened grain.*
> *I am the gentle autumn rain.*
> *When you awaken in the morning's hush*
> *I am the swift uplifting rush*
> *Of quiet birds in circled flight.*

I am the soft stars that shine at night.
Do not stand at my grave and cry;
I am not there. I did not die.

It helped me to get through many of the tough days of grieving. I share this poem because maybe it will come in handy one day for you.

Chapter Twenty

SERENDIPITY

"Sometimes what you're looking for comes when you're not looking at all."

— Fiona Childs

SEVERAL MONTHS BEFORE Robert's passing, my mom called me to say she'd met some lovely people at her church in Sacramento who had a daughter living in San Diego. Her name was Kate, and she owned a private practice physical therapy clinic. I hadn't gotten to know many people in San Diego outside my work environment, so I agreed it wouldn't hurt to spread my social wings.

Kate and I traded a few phone calls before we finally met for a quick drink after work one night. I found her to have an ebullient personality, as well as to be extremely focused and passionate about her company. Although she was busy running her clinic, and I was in the middle of Robert's illness and my job at TheraTx, we continued to meet as our schedules permitted.

During these visits, Kate disclosed to me that her private practice was struggling, and she was considering selling it to one of the corporate physical therapy businesses hoping to grow their nationwide network of clinics. One day, she called me to say she was going to Nashville to meet with an interested party.

Kate knew less than nothing about financial statements and determining the valuation of companies, so I told her to gather the previous three years of financials and meet me at my apartment that night. As I poured through balance sheets and P&Ls, Kate entertained me with stories about everything from her business to her family.

A few hours later, I shook my head and told Kate that her company was in bad shape. I advised her to make the trip, learn as much as she could about the interested investor, write down all their questions, promise forthcoming answers, and then get home and get back to work.

In the meantime, I was engulfed in doing my part to get TheraTx moved to Atlanta. Once Robert was gone, I knew I wasn't going to stay with the company, but I had no idea what I was going to do next. Then—toward the end of the company move—Kate contacted me with a proposal.

What if I handled the business and financial side of her business so she could focus on the clinical side? Keep in mind, I had scrutinized her financial statements and had a clear understanding of how dire the situation was, and I didn't know anything about the business of physical therapy. Kate's proposal came as a surprise to me, but I thought it couldn't hurt to explore the possibilities.

Once I wrapped things up at TheraTx, I started spending my days at Kate's clinic, attempting to get my arms around the business model and the underlying opportunities moving forward. Two weeks later, I sat down with Kate and advised her that I was willing to join, based on these contingencies:

1. I would commit to one year. At the end of that year, we would be back on our feet and 50/50 business partners, or we would

sell the business, split the proceeds, and go our separate ways.

2. I would infuse $10,000 into the company to create some much-needed cash flow, and the two of us would not take a salary for the next year.

3. She would handle the clinical side of the business, and I would deal with everything else.

4. It was going to be a bloodbath, so she needed to be ready for—and accepting of—disruptive changes.

Kate embraced most of my proposal, except the disruptive-changes part, because she knew I was going to let people go and make adjustments that would be uncomfortable and unpleasant. She thought about it for a few days before fully committing to a year.

We buckled up for what was going to be a wild ride. And so here I was. I had landed square in the middle of entrepreneurship. I had wanted to own my own business my entire adult life, and my first taste of it was potentially a shit sandwich.

We dove right in.

Kate put her head down to fine-tune the clinical aspects of the business, while I rolled up my sleeves and sat down with all the existing employees to determine who stayed and who needed to go. In my judgment, two employees were worth keeping; the rest needed to be weeded out over time.

From there, it became profit and loss restructuring, painfully working to dwindle down the expenses to get the bottom line out of the red zone. Nothing was sacred. Every overhead item was a potential candidate for the chopping block. Arduous and frank conversations were had with employees and vendors.

The company culture transitioned from merrymaking to unwavering value-added service to patients, a commitment to excellence, and, eventually—money-making. As grueling as it was, I was proud of what we were accomplishing. This is what Harvard Business School had trained me to do. Step-by-step, day-by-day, we managed to bring this company out of the ditch and back to life.

Exactly one year to the day after we began this expedition, we became profitable. We had a fresh team focused and passionate about their position in the company. We had forged collaborative relationships with our vendors, and our patients were receiving individualized, state-of-the-art care.

We had a tiny bit of breathing room, and Kate and I paid ourselves for the first time in 365 days. My first romp in the fields of entrepreneurship was gritty, punishing, and all-consuming. But all our blood, sweat, and tears eventually led to a moment of celebration, which made it all worth it. That said, once we had created a profitable business model with the proper people and processes in place, I needed something else to do.

Pause and Reflect: It's Already There

Not too long ago on my drive to my office, I was reflecting on my morning meditation. During this pre-dawn time of contemplation, what clearly came to me was "it is already there." Over and over again I heard this. I wasn't exactly sure what it meant, but I liked the idea a lot. And then it came to me.

All that I had accomplished in my life was already in existence before I met the experience of it. Years ago, I had the desire and the vision to own a gym that offered fitness classes and personal training. It was located in a warehouse-type building with a roll-up door and access to the outside.

People would come to maintain or evolve their physical health and wellness and to enjoy the camaraderie of like-minded folks. In exactly two hours, I would be leading a group of individuals through an hour-long functional fitness class in the gym that I owned—roll-up door and all.

I was in the midst of a lightbulb moment. The realization that I was in the experience of something that I had manifested many years ago struck me. Then, I began to look back at other incarnations of things that I had once fancied and envisioned that have revealed themselves into my reality.

For example, years ago, in my mind's eye, I held the vision of owning a home in the community in which I now reside. My vision of this desire existed long before my realization of it. As I contemplated this idea even more, the notion of "it is already there" has been a steadfast truth throughout my entire life.

From leaving the farm where I grew up, to traveling, to going to Harvard, to becoming an entrepreneur, to the home where I live, to the vehicle that I drive, and everything in between, it has all been there, unwearyingly anticipating my coming to know it.

I believe the same is valid for you. All that you desire is already there. As you reflect back on your life, you might already recognize this. Our culture is heavy on reason and knowledge, which is prized over intuition and imagination. I believe it to be wise to be reasonable and knowledgeable, but don't let it keep you from moving forward in a direction that lights you up.

Just like my first prospect of becoming an entrepreneur, none of these "already there"s appeared when I thought they would or in the manner that I had conjured up, and every single one of them commanded the best of me to show up for the event, sometimes more of me than I knew existed.

Here is the beauty of that: if going into these situations I had known the demands of getting to the other side of them, it is likely that I would have passed them up. I ask that you consider the power and potential that lies in the concept of "it is already there."

It doesn't mean that getting to it will be struggle free or clear-cut. It will require you to get off your ass and get into action. But there is nothing like knowing something for the second time.

Chapter Twenty-One

HEAL THYSELF AND THEN OTHERS

"Invention is by its very nature disruptive. If you want to be understood at all times, then don't do anything new."
— Jeff Bezos

ONE OF THE rituals that allowed me to get through the rigors of the previous year was consistent exercise. That said, while it was a lifesaver, my bad knees were starting to rebel against my fitness routine. I had patellofemoral dysfunction, meaning the kneecap (patella) doesn't track correctly with the thigh bone (femur), causing excruciating knee pain around and under the patella.

Kate—being one of the best physical therapists in the country—helped to alleviate my pain by taping my knee with a method called McConnell taping. But the tape job was extremely tough for me to re-create on my own, and after twenty minutes of working out, the tape would loosen and my knee pain would reoccur, which was beyond annoying.

"Kate, is this how all patients with my same knee challenges are treated?" "Yes, why?" she asked. "Because it sucks, and we need to change it." And boom, there it was—our next project. I found something else to do. That night, Kate and I sat down with our inventor's notebook and started hashing out how we could fix one of the most common orthopedic challenges in the world (one in four people will suffer from this distressing malady at some point in their life).

Kate taught me the anatomy of the knee and explained the mechanics of the joint. She showed me what caused patellofemoral knee pain and what needed to happen to take the pain away. I loved it. Having grown up on a farm, my ability to absorb the mechanical particulars necessary to remedy this medical anomaly was easy for me to grasp. And, I was hell-bent on solving an awful knee problem millions of people were suffering from all over the world.

We were off and running with another entrepreneurial adventure that put us knee-deep—no pun intended—into becoming inventors. Neither Kate nor I had any prior experience designing and patenting a product. However, one of the orthopedic surgeons we worked with had a friend who had a handful of inventions under his belt.

We met with him and determined it would be advantageous to bring him on as a business partner. Several weeks later, we had started a new company, hired a patent attorney, and developed several prototypes of our product. The solution to eliminating patellofemoral pain was to figure out a way to move the kneecap back into an anatomically correct and fixed position at the end of the femur bone.

We did that by fabricating a four-piece knee-brace system that consisted of a tape patch, a neoprene cuff and strap, and a muscle stimulator. Our invention became known as the OnTrack® System, and shortly became recognized as the most effective nonsurgical cure for a pervasive and vexing knee problem. We performed our clinical trials and made the brace available to several independent clinical research experts so that they could execute impartial and objective tests of their own.

Compared to the hundreds of knee braces sold by hundreds of

orthopedic product distributors in the world, the OnTrack® proved to be the most effective by far. Three hardworking and resolute individuals in San Diego, California, had introduced a product that would soon disrupt the overcrowded knee-brace market.

Chapter Twenty-Two

TOLD YOU SO. SINCERELY, YOUR GUT.

"Deep down you already know the truth."

— Anonymous

IT WOULD TAKE more than just the three of us to get the OnTrack® out to the people who so desperately needed our help. So, I immediately got to work to learn how to put a nationwide sales force together to aid in our brace distribution. We steadily added sales representatives until we had over 150 reps in thirty-eight states.

This meant Kate and I often traveled as we built our support network across the United States. For the second time in my life, I became a road warrior. Travel is a marvelous way to see the many slices of life that exist in our great country, and we met a whole lot of remarkable people, some who remain friends to this day. The downside is that it makes it hard to stay connected with those in our home community.

Inventing a patentable product is tricky enough, let alone the arduous path of manufacturing and branding the product and building a distribution model that's efficient and effective.

Launching a new business is not for the lighthearted. Owning your own company is like having a child, especially in the early stages of development. It demands copious amounts of time and energy. There are no days off, no two-week vacation every year, no holidays or half-days of work.

There's a high risk of failure. Three out of four venture-backed start-ups fail, and ninety-five percent fall short on preliminary projections. You juggle many roles, burn the candle at both ends, and shoulder heavy responsibility as you manage customers, employees, and setbacks. It takes a whole lot of guts to step into the arena with competitors who are multinational organizations with hundreds of millions (if not billions) of dollars in annual sales.

But that is precisely what we did. On more than one occasion we stared fear in the face and said, "Not today." As we were assembling our sales team and traveling around the country, we soon discovered there was no definitive treatment protocol being practiced by physical therapists to remedy patellofemoral dysfunction.

I also realized physical therapists are required to participate in continuing education courses each year in order to maintain their professional license, which was excellent news for us. I told Kate we should develop a course teaching how to treat patellofemoral dysfunction successfully, allowing us to introduce the OnTrack® brace to physical therapists all over the world.

We started an international continuing education company. We designed the course, jumped through hoops to get the credentialing and certifications we needed, and started teaching—all while still running our private practice. During all this, I realized the one thing I enjoyed most was making a positive impact on people's lives. Having been trained at one of the most capitalistic schools in the world, I knew there were a lot of ways to make money.

During that year of watching people's lives change for the better, I decided any business I was involved in from here forward would positively serve others. Service to others would be my number-one criterion for any business I would be part of for the rest of my life.

Once the knee brace and continuing education companies were both up and running, Kate and I would spend the next four years of our lives working seven days a week. We spent Monday through Friday in our physical therapy business—Kate treating patients, me handling the operations and management of the other two companies.

We'd then travel Friday to somewhere in the United States to teach our seminar for ten hours on Saturday, then fly back home Sunday to prepare and start the whole process over again Monday morning. Our efforts were paying off, as we were getting a lot of recognition for the OnTrack® and our seminars in national publications, universities, and well-known medical institutions.

Then, of course, some of our competitors started to take notice of these two gals from California who were quietly making a dent in the orthopedic-bracing space. So much so that one day I got a call from a gentleman with ties to a very significant international orthopedic products company wanting to see if we'd be interested in licensing our OnTrack® product with them. Gut instinct—I knew we should never have entertained this invitation. But we did.

One meeting led to another, then several others, and nine months later we'd crafted a deal with a company that had promised to take the OnTrack® brace and our educational seminars to the next level. After all, we were supposedly teaming up with a diverse health-care conglomerate with operations across the globe, which employed over 16,000 in over 100 countries.

What could possibly go wrong? Back to that gut instinct. The entire time we were in negotiations with the top executives, my gut told me we shouldn't trust them. There was an underlying lack of belief in what they were saying to us. Almost all the people we dealt with were arrogant and slimy.

They promised they could dramatically increase our brace sales and distribution all over the world, and easily and efficiently set up our continuing education seminars. The problem? They were not aligned with our values. Kate and I wanted to help as many people with a debilitating knee condition as we could.

Throughout our U.S. travels, we had witnessed people's lives change right before our eyes. Our treatment method would rid patients of their knee pain immediately, allowing them to do things in their lives they otherwise wouldn't be able to do. These people laughed, cried, hugged us, and often danced with joy. We made a difference in their lives that, in many cases, changed their lives forever.

Every day, when our feet hit the floor, we intended to make someone's life better. Our goal in teaching physical therapists how to treat this perplexing orthopedic predicament was to help them help their patients happily put their feet on the floor. We wanted them to become an extension of us in helping their patients conquer this pervasive, hampering knee problem.

After we signed the license agreement with company X, we went through months of a demanding transition to transfer our manufacturing, distribution, and seminar business under their umbrella. During this process, it became evident the bureaucratic, slow-moving culture they operated from was the complete antithesis of ours. We were racehorses. We got things done with no excuses.

We donned our metaphoric superhero capes every day, aiming to serve others and take their pain away. They sat behind their big, beautiful desks, buzzing for their assistants each time they needed a cup of coffee or a glass of water. They sat in large conference rooms, giggling about their latest acquisition. They played a lot of golf and told a lot of lies to us, their wives, shareholders, and each other.

Kate and I met with the transition team often and expressed our concerns about the lackluster performance. Each time, they said they would soon have everything in good order and it would be smooth sailing. Again, my gut told me "smooth sailing" was something we'd never experience with this group of corporate slugs.

On our own, we were working our asses off and making a significant dent in orthopedics and physical therapy education. Even after we joined forces with company X, we continued to work our asses off. We traveled throughout Europe and taught our course, met with international research gurus, introducing the OnTrack® brace.

We continued to trek through the United States, educating as many people as we could about a product that changed lives, but—amidst it all—we witnessed the slow decline of what we had significantly sacrificed to create. We'd given up the freedom to run our company in a way that made it successful.

We'd given up control of our education company, which led to dwindling numbers of physical therapists seeking to take our course. Worst of all, we gave up our sales force, who had stood by our sides as we built the distribution system to get the OnTrack® in the hands of people who desperately needed it.

Our sales reps were some of the most dedicated, hardworking people we'd ever known. They were loyal and resolute in helping us help others. Even though they understood why we decided to license the OnTrack®, none of them wanted us to do the deal with company X.

They cautioned us that the outcome could be disastrous. They were right. And so was my gut. Even though the agreement we signed had teeth in their performance requirements, eighteen months into our relationship, they started maneuvering to shelve the OnTrack®.

They lowered the commissions they were paying their sales reps, they stopped setting up seminars, and, ultimately, they discontinued paying the agreed-upon royalties stipulated in the license agreement. Throughout my whole life, any time I've not trusted my gut, I've gotten my ass kicked.

My hesitation in doing the deal with company X was no exception. In essence, we'd sold our soul to the devil. They gave us no choice but to sue them. For the next nine months, we spent time with attorneys preparing our case, sitting through depositions, getting deposed, and going through a lengthy mediation. Lawsuits are nasty business.

I recall sitting in a conference room next to one of our attorneys as he questioned the president of company X. The inquiry was so uncomfortable I wanted to leave the room to seek relief from the antagonistic dive into this person's private life. I sat through Kate's deposition while company X's attorney grilled her to the point of her having to leave the room to vomit.

During my testimony, I answered questions for two and a half days from the same attorney who got Kate to throw up. He asked questions with such disdain, I wondered if every cell in his body was marinating in anger. My undaunted demeanor pissed him off so much he threw a whole stack of papers in the air, which we both watched land on the space of the table that separated us.

I calmly observed his vile behavior as he awkwardly did his best to gather the scattered pages, at the same time attempting to get his holier-than-thou attorney shit together. He never looked me in the eye again. After going through the depositions, both sides agreed we would do mediation instead of going through full-blown litigation.

It would be faster and less costly. The mediator assigned to our case was a retired judge. In my humble opinion, he should have stayed retired—from everything. This guy was old, grumpy, and tired. On more than one occasion, I watched as he nodded off during testimonies.

It was evident he was not following the intricacies of the case, as both sets of attorneys had to repeat information and continually clarify their points. For two weeks, I sat in a conference room on the 26th floor of an office building in downtown San Diego and witnessed one of the most appalling displays of bullshit I'd ever seen.

One after the other, company X executives and employees sat before a judge and told everything but the truth. So help me God, I couldn't believe what I was hearing. Putting their hand on a Bible and swearing to tell the truth meant nothing to these people. It was all I could do to sit in my chair and appear to remain calm because, on the inside, I was lit up.

During a break, I expressed my dismay to our attorneys and they merely shook their head and said to get used to it, it happens all the time. I despised walking into that room each day. It was cold enough to hang meat, or so hot one could hardly breathe.

The room reeked of fabrications and deception, and Hollywood had nothing on the cast of characters who showed up every day to pull the wool over the eyes of a senile judge. Every night I went home and stood in the shower letting the hottest water I could tolerate wash the filth of the day off my soul.

In the end, we prevailed. Even the doddering judge couldn't look past the countless evidence that proved company X, its executive team, and a handful of its employees purposely didn't live up to the obligations they'd agreed to twenty-four months earlier.

I learned that I could defend myself from some bad behavior, but there was no way to protect myself from pretenders. The paramount lesson I learned: trust my gut. None of this would have happened if I had listened carefully to my intuition. From the first meeting, they smelled of deceit. To their credit, though, their behavior was consistent. Always egotistical, always slippery.

We ended up getting the OnTrack® back, but, unfortunately, we never recovered from the debilitating decision to license the product. By the time we were able to re–set up our manufacturing and attempt to create a distribution team, we'd lost enough momentum and recognition in the marketplace that we merely limped along. We continue to provide the OnTrack® System, and it remains the most effective treatment method for managing patellofemoral pain.

You can learn more about it at: www.ontrackbrace.com

Pause and Reflect: Trust Your Gut

I invite you to use your instincts. We all have access to that part inside of us that seems to know the right thing to do. Trust it. It provides the unspoken truth that deserves the honor of our close attention. Take heed of the notions you get. It will save you time, energy, effort, resources, and maybe even your life.

Trusting your gut takes practice. Some people are born with a strong intuition, and they learn to rely on its wisdom and accuracy and use it to their advantage every day. Others are stuck in their self-doubt and lack of awareness, which can be paralyzing and dangerous.

One of the most valuable skills that I can encourage you to hone is your intuition. Self-doubt comes from a lack of confidence in yourself and your abilities. It can often come from beliefs that you are unworthy or that you don't matter. I am telling you right now that permitting yourself to feel undeserving or not good enough is going to keep you trapped in relationships and situations that are damaging and debilitating and that create all kinds of havoc in your life.

I know this to be true. On many occasions in my life, I have known the right thing to do, the right thing to say, and the right place to be, and yet, I vetoed this certainty only to find myself in the throes of a shitstorm. If you have a reliable gut, count your blessings and march on with appreciation, knowing that you carry inside of you an ever-present and dependable ally.

If your hunches need some firming up, start listening to the inner dialogue that you have with yourself. Ask for guidance and then pay close attention to counsel that you receive. The best way I can describe knowing that you can trust your gut is that with it comes calm and ease. When you go against its savvy advice, you will feel anxious and maybe even irritable. You can keep yourself out of a heap of hassle by sharpening your instincts. Stop refusing to know what you already know.

Chapter Twenty-Three

Serial Entrepreneur

"The best way to predict the future is to create it."
— Peter Drucker

IN THE MIDST of our challenges with company X, Kate (same name, different Kate), a dear friend of mine who handled the billing department for our physical therapy practice, called me to say she couldn't see herself sitting behind a desk staring at a computer for the rest of her working life.

She wanted to figure out a way to create more income for herself and her family. I told her to go home that night and find something in her life that was broken and figure out a way to fix it. Seemingly, an overnight solution to some annoying inconvenience is highly unlikely, but she called me the very next day and said she'd figured it out.

While cleaning up after dinner, she reached into her food-storage-container drawer and frustratingly couldn't find a matching lid to the bowl she wanted to use. The age-old maddening challenge of not having matching covers and bowls in one's so-called "Tupperware drawer."

Kate then explained to me that, in her frustration, she all of a sudden came up with a way to snap all of the same-sized lids together, which would then connect to the bottom of the matching bowls. Also, the various sizes would nest inside of one another from largest to smallest, making storage simple and convenient. Brilliant!

Within twenty-four hours of our first conversation, Kate had fashioned the answer to a widespread household problem that would help millions of people get organized. Since I'd been through the patent and trademark process with the OnTrack®, Kate asked if I would help her walk through the copious steps involved in applying for, and eventually obtaining, the intellectual property rights to protect her idea.

So, once again, I committed to stepping into the arena of continued entrepreneurship, fully aware of the land mines that existed on a trek to triumph. The first step in our expedition was to hire a patent attorney who would hopefully craft a bulletproof document keeping likely copycats from pilfering our technology.

Once that was done, we needed to come up with a catchy name for the product that would be easily brandable. I suggested Snap-Saver, The No Brainer Container®. Done. We settled on the name and immediately trademarked it.

We didn't want to go to the expense and risk involved in designing the product, building prototypes, creating molds, and all of the other components required for Snap-Saver® to become a reality, so we decided to seek a license agreement with one of the companies already in the business.

You read it right: after having gone through my messy involvement in a license agreement, it seemed to be the path of least resistance. I have said on more than one occasion, *"If you lose, don't lose the lesson."* Every experience contains a gift if we allow ourselves to step back and let the gift find its way to the surface.

My experience of going through the licensing route with the OnTrack® had taught me a lot. Kate and I began to research the corporations that were global players in the food storage container market—those who had generated over $450 million in annual revenues in the United States.

One by one, we developed profile sheets for each of these companies, learning as much as we could about everything from the financial structure, to the leadership team, to the company philosophy. Once we filed our patent application and received our patent pending status, we began to contact each of these companies, introducing our technology and inquiring as to their interest in entering into a license agreement with Snap-Saver.

We corresponded with twenty-six organizations who we felt would be a good fit for what we wanted to accomplish. We got some nibbles from a handful of these sought-after potential licensors. After many months of back-and-forth conversation and information exchanges, the top three vendors in the United States—all of whom were global players in the food storage space—were interested in further discussions with us.

We entered into negotiations with each of these entities. The number one player (who, by the way, still holds the top position in the market) eventually stepped away from the bargaining table, stating they would not commit to the required guaranteed royalty minimums and sales hurdles.

The real reason—as we read between the lines—was that they paid a lot of money to an in-house development team responsible for coming up with the latest and greatest in food storage. In other words, "If we didn't think of it, it isn't worth anything." A bit arrogant, don't you think? The other two players ultimately dropped out of the negotiations as well, due to dramatic organizational restructuring and changing business strategies.

There we were: after almost two years of chasing what seemed to be promising candidates to usher the Snap-Saver® technology into the marketplace, we had nothing. We decided to take another run at some of the second-tier companies we hadn't considered the first time around. Once again, we had some interest from a few companies that we bantered back and forth with for a few months, to no avail.

We concluded the only way to get Snap-Saver off the ground was to do it ourselves. Through business contacts, we were introduced to a fellow who had a great deal of experience and success in selling products on QVC and the Home Shopping Network.

After several meetings with him and one of his associates, we decided they could help us introduce Snap-Saver® via TV shopping. Once we negotiated our agreement with them, our next step was to raise money to hire a design team, develop prototypes, buy steel, make molds, develop short-form TV ads, and a handful of other costly-but-necessary details to launch our business.

We were entering intimidating territory. Our project was not big enough to attract venture capital investors, so we decided to offer an equity position to people we knew: business associates, friends, and family. Asking for money from individuals with whom we were close was scary. There was no promise whatsoever.

We were going up against giants in the industry, with little more than a hope and a prayer. But off we went, developing and sending a comprehensive business plan to a group of people we wanted to be part of our vision. We had long and exhausting conversations with folks, explaining our concept and our rollout strategy.

We met with some in person and others on the phone. In the end, we rallied together thirty-nine investors and raised 1.8 million dollars. The most significant investor participated to the tune of $500,000, the smallest, $10,000. Along with the money came a landslide of emotions.

Everything from gratitude to breathtaking fear. Although we had developed a concept that we were dedicated to making a great success, Kate and I felt beholden to these men and women who had risked their hard-earned money to support us in an adventure with no guarantees. Nine out of ten startups will fail. It's the harsh and dismal truth. Bleak statistics, coupled with the responsibility of being the watchful stewards of other people's money, was something Kate and I took very seriously.

We armored up to protect the investment of those who had put their trust in our mission. At the same time, we wore an emblematic leaden vest for years as we trekked through some of the most jagged landscapes that entrepreneurship and corporate America had to offer.

Chapter Twenty-Four

DAVID AND GOLIATH

"The fact of being an underdog changes people in ways that we often fail to appreciate. It opens doors and creates opportunities and educates and enlightens and permits things that might otherwise have seemed unthinkable."

— Malcolm Gladwell

DETAILING THE EXTENSIVE trials and tribulations we faced on our journey is deserving of a book all unto itself. Kate and I have pondered on more than one occasion the benefits of sharing our story. As valuable, truthful, and encouraging as it would be, neither of us has the burning desire to relive some of the most trying years of our professional life. Here is the *Reader's Digest* version.

Our design team collaborated with our manufacturing group to develop the Snap-Saver® system. We found a creative team to put together a short-form video ad to be used for our TV shopping strategy. Kate went to the QVC headquarters in Pennsylvania several times to present Snap-Saver® to the viewing audience.

All of these critical steps along the way helped us to gain traction in the marketplace. The next evolution in the induction of our product was to find our way into the retail arena. Requisite to play in this rough-and-tumble space, we gathered together packaging and distribution systems, as well as money, faith, and hope.

It also meant finding a spot on the shelf next to all our competitors in places like Costco, Target, Wegmans, and Kmart. No easy task, but we managed to nudge in next to the best in the industry. And then, after all of this, we got a phone call from one of our investors.

They had just returned home from a shopping outing where they saw what seemed to be a knockoff of our Snap-Saver® food storage containers. Disbelief. Sucker punch. *What? Are you kidding me? Can this be true? Thanks for the call. We will check into it.*

Sure enough, it appeared one of our competitors, the biggest and most well-known in the United States, had taken it upon their superior selves to infringe on our patent. You've heard the ole "innocent until proven guilty," which is the cornerstone of the American legal system, right?

Well, just as we were getting some recognition in the food storage industry, we had to go up against one of the colossal corporate titans in the world. Charles Colton once said, "Imitation is the sincerest form of flattery." Adulation and fawning from a company that seemed to be trespassing were not the emotions we were feeling at this moment.

We had no choice but to find a law firm that would agree to a contingency arrangement because we indeed did not have a treasure chest of funds to fight a behemoth with a stable full of tire-biting, in-house, and external representation. After a significant amount of digging and research, we found a firm based in Minneapolis, Minnesota, that had prior experience in prevailing over our opponent.

Lawsuits can eat up years of time and treasure. Given our underdog status, we also needed to find a state that would fast-track our case. We did: Wisconsin. It turns out, it was the state where our competitor and foe was manufacturing the alleged infringing product—finally, some good news.

We learned of the potential infringement in March. For the next several months, we were busy making copies of all of our corporate records, patent files, design materials, and correspondence from the previous six years. I don't recall the exact number of boxes of documents we sent off to our attorneys, but it took weeks to compile, organize, and bundle together.

In July of 2008, Kate and I flew to Minneapolis to sit down and comb through all the thousands of pages of materials with our attorneys. In the meantime, the court assigned a judge to our case. Our attorneys filed all the required paperwork necessary to request a summary judgment of our situation.

Based on the motion that we contended that all of the needed factual matters were so one-sided that there was no need for a full trial, the judge granted us a summary judgment. It was clear our rival had indeed infringed on our patent, so we could avoid the time and costs of preparing for a full-blown trial to prove infringement and instead, focus on determining damages and coming to a settlement agreement.

Coming to a resolution regarding damages still required us to go through many hours of depositions, meetings, and mock trials. As a client of previous lawsuits, one of the lessons I learned is that you have to manage your attorneys. They don't have nearly as much at stake, and they get paid, regardless of the outcome.

As luck would have it, we were going through the settlement process in the middle of the Christmas holiday season. The timing was strenuous, to say the least. Kate, her family, and I were growing weary of our months of involvement in this lawsuit.

Our attorneys didn't have much enthusiasm, having to work full steam through the holidays, and our investors were beyond anxious. It was challenging to keep everyone's focus on the matter at hand. A trial date was finally set for January 10.

After days of bantering back and forth with the opposing attorneys, both parties agreed to meet in Chicago three days after Christmas to see if we could hammer out an agreeable settlement without having to go to trial.

We sat around a long, wide, and wooden table in a cold, dank conference room at the Chicago Airport Hilton to begin negotiations. On our side: Kate, me, our business partner, and our attorney. On their side: the president of the home goods division, an in-house attorney, an in-house, high-ranking finance guy, and their external legal counsel.

After hours of back-and-forth debating, we came to a handshake deal around 10:00 pm. Kate and I didn't sleep at all that night, uneasy about the deal to which we had just agreed. Early the next morning, we got out of bed and decided that, in order for our investors and us to reap any reward from all the hard work we had been through with this rough-and-tumble lawsuit, we had to recraft the deal.

The only place we saw room for negotiation was with our attorneys. The contingency arrangement that had been set up allowed our attorneys to take a percentage of the deal we made with our competitors. If we didn't cap the amount we paid them, all of the investors—including ourselves—would come out with little to zero benefit.

Kate and I ran through some numbers together, then called our business partner to discuss our plan. He said, "Good luck, the attorneys will never agree to that." No support from him at all. Fortunately, one of our investors was a smart, talented, retired corporate attorney.

Kate and I picked up the phone and called to run our idea by him. He thought it was worth pursuing and dictated the language we should use to amend our contingency agreement. We were supposed to reconvene with the other side late morning to finalize the deal we had agreed upon the night before, so time was of the essence to meet with our attorney and present the change in the contingency agreement.

Although he and his firm were going to make a big chunk of money for the six months' worth of work they had done for us, this change was not going to be well-accepted. We arranged to meet him in a coffee shop. Kate and I would soon hand across the table a controversial piece of paper to a man who had represented us for the past 180 days.

Before we left our hotel room, I told Kate to be brave, to be brief with her words, and to sit emotionless, without saying another word, while he read the words on the page. I would do the same. As we approached our destination, we heard the clanking of dishes and the quiet rumble of multiple conversations happening at the same time.

In the corner, we spotted our guy sitting with a cup of coffee, reading the *Wall Street Journal*. He stood up and greeted us with a smile, not knowing things were about to change. After a brief exchange of pleasantries, Kate cleared her throat and began her short, concise presentation.

As instructed, she then sat back with stable posture as we waited. After reading what Kate handed him, his hand slammed down on the table, sending forks and knives flying into the air, tumbling to the ground with a pinging thud. Coffee cups rattled in their saucers, outwardly expressing what we felt inside.

The other patrons in the cafe stopped and stared as our guy yelled. He angrily told us we were the most miserable clients he'd ever had, that our case had been a complete pain in his ass from the beginning, and that he couldn't wait to rid his life of us.

We weren't expecting high compliments from him, but we didn't anticipate a full-on temper tantrum laced with flowery language in the middle of a public venue. Kate and I did as we had promised each other we would do: sat there expressionless on the outside, stunned and uncomfortable on the inside.

We watched as his blood pressure peaked, then slowly came down as his face went from billion-dollar red to a flushed pink. We sat still as he attempted to collect himself and recover from his explosive display of surprise and frustration. Those around us slowly went back to their breakfast and conversation that had been abruptly interrupted only minutes earlier.

Our guy began to gather together his paper, briefcase, and overcoat. Kate and I still hadn't spoken a word. He stood up and said he needed to call his managing partner to discuss the change we had presented him. Then he stormed away, leaving a coffee shop and two women who breathed a palpable sigh of relief.

Forty-five uneasy minutes later, our attorney contacted us and informed us he had spoken to his law firm's managing partner, who had agreed to our fee proposal. Relieved, Kate and I passed the news on to our once-skeptical business partner. A few hours later, we were back in that lackluster conference room where the negotiations had started the day before.

The attorneys nailed down the specifics of the deal, and we wrapped up two days of emotional anguish. We got to the airport just in time to wolf down some McDonald's French fries—unquestionably a suitable reward for such grueling work—and caught our flight home.

The next several months entailed communicating with investors and transitioning Snap-Saver from a manufacturing and distribution company to one that received quarterly royalties as its sole revenue source. As I mentioned previously, bookstores across the world house tomes narrating the details of similar experiences that take place in the world of business. For now, this is the extent to which our story exists. The future of this could possibly change, but the central theme of this bump in the Snap-Saver road is that the unexpected glitch in our journey was a gift.

Our adversary-turned-ally was a leading global consumer goods company. They had a distribution network second to none, and they retroactively paid us royalties on all sales they had made using our infringed-upon technology, as well as all future sales until our patent expired.

The unforeseen event furnished us with the chance to pay off all our expenses and make distributions to our investors that ended up surpassing their original investment by 1.75 times. After we paid back the initial investments, Kate and I were able to participate in the royalty distributions, making for a handsome income for several years. Entrepreneurship is like that.

We worked for ten years on Snap-Saver® before we saw one dime in reward. Kate and I didn't rest peacefully until we erased all of our debt and made our investors whole. Being responsible for other people's money is a burden. Although each of these stakeholders knew the possibility existed that they could lose some or all of their outlay, they took the risk.

They signed legal documents stating their understanding of the gamble in which they were engaging. These papers released Snap-Saver of any liability should our company perish in our endeavor. None of this lessened the heaviness of the self-imposed obligation Kate and I felt to be good stewards of their money.

Through the final distribution, we took great care in managing the company in a manner that had integrity and transparency.

Pause and Reflect: It's a Lot Like Farming

Like farming, there are no guarantees when it comes to entrepreneurship. It's risky business. Like farming, there are seasons. Sometimes years of spring and summer go by before reaping the rewards.

There are high highs as well as excruciating lows. There are moments of great pride and moments of questioning just about everything. Free enterprise is not something you chase; it's something you choose. In a way, it took me back to my roots. Instead of being at the helm of a very substantial piece of equipment with duty beyond my years, we looked around and asked, "What's broken?" Then we did what we could to fix it.

Chapter Twenty-Five

———— ∾∾ ————

THE BEGINNING OF THE END

"You're not sorry you did it, you're sorry I found out."
— Unknown

IN JANUARY OF 2007, I was going about my usual Sunday chores of feeding horses and cleaning up around the barn while enjoying a sunny winter day on my little sliver of heaven in Rancho Santa Fe, California. My cell phone rang. I noted that it was my brother Dan calling.

I was in the middle of scooping horseshit, so I didn't answer, making a mental note to call him later that afternoon. Within five minutes, my phone rang again, and again, it was Dan. This was out of character for him. Usually, if I didn't answer, he would leave me a message to call him back.

My gut told me something wasn't right, so I answered. "Hey, what's going on?" His voice, serious and somber, replied, "You're not going to believe this; George is dead." Those words stopped me cold. I had never thought about getting that call. It had been years since I had spoken to George, let alone thought about him dying. I didn't think about him much at all.

It was fifteen years earlier that George decided he was ready to quit farming. Just like that, one day he just up and decided he was prepared to throw in his John Deere towel. This abrupt decision was disruptive, inconvenient, and unfortunate timing for Dan and his family. Dan loved the farm, he was passionate about farming, and he cherished his small but mighty family.

At the time, Dan was working on the road doing construction as a way to make a living. He was in Atlanta, Georgia, when he got the call from George telling him that he needed to get home and sign the paperwork to purchase the farm. Even though Dan would be back in two weeks, that was too long for George to wait.

I don't know what the big rush was, but George had a hair across his ass, and he was adamant about the urgency of getting this deal done. Dan's focus was on making a living to provide for his family, and at the same time, his true desire was to farm, so he got on a plane and flew home.

He signed the paperwork, got back on a plane, and went back to Atlanta. Two weeks later, he wrapped up his construction job and came home to start the next chapter of his life. As it turned out, the reason for the rush was because George had slanted the deal ridiculously far in his favor.

He knew—because of Dan's swift trip—he wouldn't have time to review the details of the agreement. Plus, Dan wasn't savvy with this type of business transaction. He trusted that prior conversations with George about his interest in buying the farm would be honored.

The ink had barely dried on the contract when Dan contacted me shortly after he settled on the farm and said he just couldn't abide by the terms of the deal. I asked him to mail me a copy of the agreement so I could see for myself what was going on. I don't remember the details of the paperwork, but I do remember that, even before I got through the entire document, my blood was boiling.

I was stunned and appalled. How does someone intentionally screw over their own flesh and blood? This farm is where we grew up. It was the farm George's parents had carved out for him, hoping he would keep it in the family forever. It was the farm we were slaves to for most of our childhood.

And yet, it was the farm that made us who we are. So, I called George. One of the first things I remember saying to him was, "By the time we finish with this conversation, you may wish you never even THOUGHT about having me." I strongly suggested he craft a new deal with Dan. One that was fair and reasonable, and the sooner he did this, the better.

I also threw in the threat that one of my attorneys would contact him to explain the wisdom in my proposal. Without many words from him, we hung up. In less than thirty minutes, Dan called me saying George had left him a message to renegotiate the farm deal. In the end, Dan and George worked out a sensible arrangement. I hammered a proverbial nail in the coffin. That was it. I was done with George.

Chapter Twenty-Six

WHAT ARE THE CHANCES?

"Sometimes things fall apart so that better things can fall together."
— Marilyn Monroe

THE DEATH OF George changed me. That, coupled with a lawsuit, a failed relationship, and my house burning to the ground, kicked my ass. It was October 22, 2007, in Rancho Santa Fe, California. The day was ushered in at 4:30 am with a reverse 911 call, informing me of a required evacuation.

A fire had started the previous afternoon in a community about forty miles from my home. It was aggressive, fast-moving, and headed my way. I immediately woke up Gene—the man who I had been in a long-term relationship with—and my tenant, who was renting my guesthouse.

I told my tenant to gather his possessions together, focusing on things he valued most, and find somewhere to go. It was likely this fire was going to destroy everything in its path. I convinced Gene to go to the barn with me and hook up the horse trailer to load with as many of our personal belongings as it could hold.

We had no way of knowing when we would be back. I immediately started wrapping cherished paintings in packing blankets and taking them to the trailer. I was deliberate and focused as I purposely grabbed what I considered to be beloved possessions that, if lost, couldn't be replaced.

Gene helped me with a few paintings, mostly those that were "his"; then he stood around, watching me gather what I could fit into my Ranger Rover or the trailer. He didn't think my house was going to be destroyed, but I knew in my gut this cherished place I called home would perish in this oncoming firestorm.

I gathered up my dogs, fed my horses, and prayed they would survive the trauma of this random act of nature that was fiercely making its way toward the canyons surrounding my house and barn. On the way to work, I called my friend and neighbor, Lynn, to tell her we had evacuated and I had chosen to leave my horses in the corral, knowing it was their best chance at survival.

She and her husband Rick had decided to stay and do all they could to keep their property from burning. I was understandably distracted during the day, glued to the news reports of the status of the fire. Internally, I was fighting a battle of knowingness in my gut vs. the desire for a positive outcome in my head.

Lynn checked in with me throughout the day, keeping me posted on what was going on in real-time. She could see my house from the high knoll, several hundred yards from her front door. At 4:38 pm, Lynn called me for the last time that day. My gut won the hard-fought battle. My house was on fire.

I left my office and made my way to Lynn and Rick's house. I traveled the backroads, watching fire cut a wide swath of destruction for miles through the hills around me, praying the entire time that, when I was able to get to my three horses, the worst-case scenario would be they were hungry.

After three attempts to get to the barn, each met with a massive wall of fire taking siege of the canyon and surrounding my property; we were finally able to get to my corral. We found three horses. My horses. And they were ALIVE. And hungry, so I fed them. While Lynn and I wiped ash and dirt out of the horses' eyes and noses, Rick and Gene gathered up a few garden hoses and managed to get onto the roof of the barn to wet it down, hoping to keep any flying embers from landing on it and sparking more fire. The wind was blowing seventy to eighty miles an hour, switching direction every few minutes. We were standing in the middle of an ominous firestorm that was acting like an uncaged monster. Palm trees were exploding; propane tanks were blowing up, adding more fuel to the raging flames.

I could hear rounds of ammunition going off—not because someone was firing a weapon, but because ammo left behind by evacuees was discharging from the heat of the inferno. I don't know what a war zone is like, but I was as close to one as I ever wanted to be.

I held on to the fence to steady myself against the unrelenting wind and watched my house burn to the ground. Except for the few things Gene and I had removed earlier that morning, I witnessed every single possession I owned get swallowed up by an angry beast. Just like that—forty-seven years of me turned into a pile of ash.

I will never forget what it looked like watching my life go up in flames. There are just some things that leave an indelible impression on a person. I never felt like a fire victim, even though that label was being handed out like Halloween candy. I wasn't willing to let this circumstance, this situation, define my life.

The way I figured it, my house burning to the ground was all part of God's plan for me, and if the big guy wanted me to navigate through the journey of building a new house, then that was precisely what I would do. The fire burned for two more days, and by the time it was contained, it had burned 197,990 acres and destroyed 1,650 structures.

To this day, it's noted as one of the topmost destructive fires on record. I was supposed to be in Minneapolis the day after my house burned to meet with attorneys about the ongoing lawsuit involving Snap-Saver. I didn't make the trip. The days following the fire were filled with the basics like eating, figuring out where I was going to live, taking care of my animals, and gathering together the details of re-creating a significant portion of my life.

Chapter Twenty-Seven

OUT OF THE ASHES

"Yes, I will rise out of these ashes, rise from this trouble I have found. And this rubble on the ground, I will rise."
— Shawn McDonald

BUILDING A HOUSE from the ground up was never on my list of things to do. I had no idea where to start. But, as with most challenges in my life, I've found getting to the end was as simple as taking it one step at a time. I began by going through mounds of magazines, collecting photos of homes I liked.

I spent hours with a sketchbook, drawing floorplans. I researched materials on landscaping and design before meeting with an architect to explain my vision. I met with contractors and engineers, electricians and plumbers, framers and painters, concrete people and roofers. Anyone it took to create a structure I would one day call "home."

Right after my house burned to the ground, and before there was even a first pour of foundation on which to begin to build my new house, I spent seventeen long months dealing with my insurance company, attempting to obtain the myriad of permits, preparing the architectural drawings, getting approvals from local design boards, doing the grading and site work, hiring a contractor and subs.

I'd made thousands of decisions in those seventeen months and had thousands more to make before it was all over. During this time, Gene and I were attempting to untether our long and complicated relationship, and I was doing my best to fulfill my role in all of the businesses in which I was an owner.

Each day I would show up at the job site thirty minutes before quitting time to answer questions, pay people, meet with the general contractor, and, of course, make decisions. Then, I would stay to clean up so the workers could do their job without interruption until 3 pm each day.

Spending these two to three hours at the end of the day at the site allowed me the time and space to absorb the day's progress. Cleaning up gave me a chance to embrace the process, soaking up as much about building a new home as I could. It also upped my game with the workers, because they knew I was paying attention to how they performed their job.

They quickly understood I had high expectations and was astute enough not to let anything fall through the cracks. Ultimately, this daily routine not only nurtured my soul but saved me tens of thousands of dollars in labor costs and change orders. What I appreciated most about these hours of solitude was the intimacy with the land and the artisanship of creating a beautiful and safe place for me to hang my hat.

It only took eight months to complete the construction of my house. Two years and nineteen days after I watched my house go up in flames, I moved into my brand-new home. Because of a dispute with one of my vendors, there was no flooring in the house, except for the bathrooms and hallways.

I wasn't sure when the disagreement with the purveyor would conclude, so I opted to move in with an air mattress and an armload of clothes and necessities. I picked the bedroom where I felt most secure, blew up the bed, and put the sheets on it. I sat on the edge of that bed, which was only ten inches off the concrete floor, leaned forward, placing my elbows on my knees, and said to myself, "Annie, you MUST get your shit together."

Then, I reached over and gave my dog, Porkchop, a pat before falling back on the bed in pure exhaustion. It was the first time in 749 days I felt like I had a moment's reprieve from months of unyielding requirements of my time, energy, and emotion. I lived in my big, empty house with no furniture, no TV, and no distractions of any kind for an entire year.

In addition to the loss of practically all of my personal belongings, my relationship with Gene had come to a necessary, yet painful end. I decided to simply be with the loss and heartache. As humanly challenging as it was, I elected to accept all that each moment brought to me, as if I had chosen it for myself, because ultimately, I did. I was still—often. I went on many walks.

I lived moment-to-moment and realized that being happy, healed, and safe was all a matter of choice. As the days, weeks, months, and years passed, I learned a lot—about myself and others, about life and love.

Along the way (after thousands of magazine pages, a bunch of books, a seminar here and there, the support of friends and family, and absolute determination), I created "Lines in the Sand: A Ten-Step Invitation to Be Your Authentic Self." I created it because I want to help others live an authentic life. A life that is extraordinary. A life worth living.

The following tenets are the "Lines in the Sand" that I constructed for myself in the process of redesigning my life. These are the ten principles that I am committed to living by to create and maintain a life that I love.

LINE ONE: BE AUTHENTIC

Get real. This was unquestionably the number one commitment that I made to myself as I was on the march to redesign my life. I had wandered so far from my genuineness that on many occasions, I didn't even recognize myself. As difficult as it is to admit it, much of my behavior was dreadful. Straight up. Dire, disconnected, and untethered from goodness in my day-to-day living.

There is nothing like a quick kick in the ass from God to set things right. I was truly humbled by death, the loss of my home, and resigning from an unhealthy relationship. All heart-wrenching on the one hand, and incredible gifts on the other hand.

Always be brave enough to be yourself.

LINE TWO: VIEW EVERY EXPERIENCE AS A GIFT

One of the best questions that I asked myself often during my year of renewal was, "What is the gift in this?" I had to. I felt hollowed out by loss. It was as if I was made of fragile glass that even the slightest breeze could shatter into tiny pieces that could never be put back together again.

Loss of any sort is difficult. It is hard to understand, and it can make you angry and scared. However, no matter how small, look for the gift in your life experiences. Our evolved selves understand the importance of ALL of the experiences and relationships we encounter on our life journey.

LINE THREE: QUIET YOURSELF SO THAT YOU CAN HEAR THE WHISPERS OF DESTINY

During my year of revamping my life, I spent a lot of time being quiet and listening and walking and writing and reading and healing. I quickly came to appreciate that life is about what you do, not what you have.

My journey continues, and always will. I embrace this truth. The voyage that I was on was not all seashells and balloons, and there were many minutes, hours, and days that I was knee-deep in the quicksand of emotional muck. The important thing was for me to be with it, embrace it, understand it, make peace with it, and then be done with it.

Please allow yourself some quiet time each day.

LINE FOUR: EMBRACE AND PRACTICE SURRENDER

I was willing to surrender it all. I had lost so much. But you know what? I gained so much more.

Surrender is to yield power, control, or possession. Letting go lets in happiness. Being present in the moment and simply accepting it for what it is, although challenging, gives you freedom from pain.

When we allow our identity to be attached to what we own, who we date or marry, or our circle of friends, we are not being our authentic selves. We ultimately lose ourselves because we are relying on these things and people for our sense of worth. There is tremendous freedom in "letting go." So, do yourself a favor: liberate yourself from the people, places, and things that steal your truth.

LINE FIVE: ASTONISH YOURSELF EVERY DAY

Before my house burned down, I traveled the same sixteen miles to my office each day and the same sixteen miles home. I don't recall ever taking time to notice anything new along the way. Why? Because I wasn't looking. I was in a rut. What I noticed about losing almost everything is that it cleared a path for me to start paying attention, to start seeing for the first time in years. I began to recognize the exquisiteness in the simplest of things.

It is hard to see clearly out of a dirty windshield. It is hard to find your desk when it is covered in unorganized chaos. It is hard to hear nature if you are talking. It is hard to experience good when you are focused only on bad. It is almost impossible to know how another feels when you don't take the time to look into their eyes. It is rare to be astonished if you are not astonishable.

Line Six: Do Right, Not Be Right

The need to be right is a symptom of the lack of self-esteem or wanting to be in control or feel superior to others. Reflect on a time when you found yourself needing to be right, and answer the following questions regarding that situation:

- *Is being right worth the time it will steal from me?*
- *What can I do to understand the person or the situation?*
- *How is my life going to be better by "being right"?*
- *What is it about my lack of self-esteem that is creating my need to be right?*

Line Seven: Be Impeccably Fiscally Fit

I encourage you to respect money and have a desire for money but never live your life for money. Research shows that those whose sole focus is money and material things are physically, emotionally, and spiritually bankrupt.

Where there is money, there is emotion. The prevalent feeling associated with money is fear. There is a fear of never having enough, fear of losing it all, fear of being judged by how much money one has or doesn't have, and the list goes on.

I have found that the best way to keep my financial fear quiet is to be impeccable with my handling of money. I have a budget, retirement plan, and a slush fund. Additionally, I have a will and a revocable living trust, and I surround myself with experts and resources to assist me in keeping my fiscal world in good order. Please do the same for yourself.

Line Eight: Live Graciously

Living in the world today presents a considerable amount of confusion and ungoverned influence. Hectic lifestyles are the norm. Consumption runs rampant, and material things seem to trump the

"less is more" philosophy. I call it the herd mentality. "Everyone is doing it so it must be worth doing ... I guess I should be doing it too."

The problem is, "it" is a fast-paced, drive-thru, instant gratification
mentality that seems to be the quest of the masses. Mindless madness
and to what end? To live graciously, we must recognize that "more isn't
always better," and we do already have all that we need. Graciousness
or grace-filled-ness is not achievable when we are overscheduled, over-
committed, and overloaded.

Only in living a graceful life can we recognize and honor the possessions that we have, appreciate the real worth of loved ones and others we care for, and value what we do.

LINE NINE: TAKE RESPONSIBILITY FOR YOU, INC.

Have you ever peered in the mirror and wondered what is deep
within the "man" or "woman" looking back at you? Have you ever been
"fooled" by the appearance of another and have you ever thought you
might be fooling yourself? Have you ever thought, is there more? Or
less?

The foundation of the ultimate life plan starts with YOU from
the inside out. It means getting back to basics. It means having an
honest conversation with yourself, about yourself. You are the Board
of Directors to You, Inc. You have the ultimate responsibility for the
success of You ... NO ONE ELSE ... ONLY YOU!

LINE TEN: MAKE A DENT

What does this whole thing "make a dent" mean anyway? How
often, if ever, does one sit and contemplate one's purpose for existing?
What is it we are supposed to do during our time on earth?

We often cling to the illusions we have been taught ... our purpose
is to have a great career, get married and have children, purchase the
house with the picket fence, get rich, climb the ladder of upward social

mobility, be a power player, or a myriad of other "surface" ideas.

I don't think our purpose has anything to do with any of those things. It is not about what we do for a living, how much money we have, or who we know. I am suggesting that the purpose of our life is to go on a journey to becoming real. A journey of living authentically and uncovering who we really are. Say it, welcome it, and be it!

Chapter Twenty-Eight

GENE

"Never sacrifice your class to get even with someone with none. Take the high road."

— Unknown

BEFORE MEETING GENE, I had dated a handful of men—all of whom were handsome, kind, and fun guys. None of these relationships lasted for more than a couple of years, primarily because I was young and on the move. After graduating from high school, I went out of state to college.

I accepted my first corporate job in the business world, which led to relocation from the Midwest to the East Coast. That led to applying and being admitted to Harvard Business School. I couldn't turn that down, so another transition. After business school, I moved to the West Coast and dove into my first post-grad position with a start-up.

The company relocated to the Southeast; I didn't—another transition. And, finally, I met one of my current business partners and began my life as an entrepreneur. Each one of these evolutions brought a mutually-agreed-upon end to a relationship—some more mutual than others.

The first time I met Gene, I was sitting at a Starbucks doing a crossword puzzle. Two guys on their road bikes rolled up, dismounted their rides, and clicked their way to the table where I was sitting alone. The more ebullient one asked if they could join me.

I said sure and introduced myself. In turn, I met John and Gene. Gene was the quiet one. We had a pleasant conversation, and thirty minutes later, the guys got on their bikes and rode into the distance. At this point in my life, my business partner and I were working in our physical therapy clinic during the week and traveling almost every weekend to promote a product we had invented.

Roughly two months after I met John and Gene, I was checking my messages between flights. There was a voicemail from Gene, asking if I'd like to go to a rodeo with him. I was taken aback because I hadn't given him my phone number. I didn't know him at all, let alone would I take the risk of going to a rodeo with him. And anyway—I had a plane to catch.

A few weeks later, I got another call—this time at my office. He'd tracked my number down through a country club membership directory of which my business partner belonged—information he had gathered months earlier during our conversation at Starbucks. He wanted to meet for coffee.

I agreed, thinking I should learn more about this guy who had gone to great lengths to pursue me. We had an enjoyable chat. The weekend bike rider had transformed into a cowboy, which was right up my alley. I learned what he did for a living, that he had a horse, and that the cowboy way inspired him.

I found him to be well-spoken, handsome in a rugged kind of way, and my type of man. He even showed me photos of his kids (there was no mention of their mother). As time went by, I still had my rigorous work and travel schedule, but I found my mind drifting to Gene.

We met a few more times for coffee, where I became more intrigued with him, and a bit enamored. At some point, I asked about his kids' mom. What was the story? It turns out he was separated. He was in an unhappy marriage; they were trying to figure out how to go their separate ways.

Once again, the details and timetable of this period are hard for me to recall with much specificity. However, what I do know is that Gene and I continued our rendezvous—meeting for coffee, going to dinner, taking long drives. I was falling for this supposedly unconnected man. I thought we were doing what most people would call "dating" and "falling in love," when, in truth, we were sneaking around.

One day, during lunch, Gene told me he was moving his elderly aunts into his guesthouse. His wife was going to be their primary caregiver, complicating things. In no uncertain terms, he told me he was no longer separated. WOW. Okay. I was out. I immediately refocused on my business, using work as my guide to ease my heartache.

However, Gene continued his pursuit. His behavior was welcomed on the one hand and confusing on the other. Even though I knew it was wrong, I would meet with him on weekend mornings, taking long drives to places where the likelihood of running into anyone we knew was slim.

I fell back in—hook, line, and sinker—and held on to Gene's promise that, as soon as his aunts (who were not in good health) passed, he would be free to execute his plan of leaving his so-called "miserable" marriage. This is the moment I parted ways with my "North Star."

I flat out ditched my authenticity and became a person I often didn't recognize as myself. I spit in the face of who I was deep inside; I unwittingly discarded my truth, trading it in for what would unfold as a dance with malice. For the second time in my life, I found myself in the clutches of a narcissist. And, my ass was completely "out of the saddle."

After all kinds of ugliness and spectacle, Gene did leave his marriage, spending years navigating through emotional strife with his bitter ex-wife and pissed-off kids. Looking back on the events, the twists and turns of a marriage ending, it is now easy to understand the effects of this unfortunate upheaval. It was hard for everyone involved, and no one came out unscathed in some way.

Gene and I continued our relationship. Many things made our bond compatible: we had very similar preferences when it came to food, decor, travel, animals, and good health. I learned a lot from him. He introduced me to art, real estate, new friends and experiences. We had some magnificent times together, and I will always appreciate those occasions.

Regrettably, I spent the bulk of my long relationship with Gene cavorting between feeling unsafe and knowing in my gut I was in a situation that was not right for me. Even though I loved Gene very much, I acknowledge now that his love for me was conditional. It was all part of a self-absorbed personality.

I don't share this information to bash men. I love and admire men, and I'm privileged to know many males who are beautiful examples of husbands, fathers, and friends. I disclose these particulars to help you discern the nuances of egotistical behavior.

My feelings of self-doubt, dismay, mistrust, and unease were real, and they lasted through the duration of our relationship. Because Gene overvalued himself, he spent a great deal of time devaluing me. The fact that I went to Harvard bothered him. Regardless of how triumphant I was in any aspect of my life or what I accomplished, he was always better in some way, and he reminded me of this often.

It was common practice for Gene to pick a fight and turn the tables on me, as if it was my fault, then completely ignore me for days as punishment. I was talked to and treated in ways I would never have conceived, and Gene expected me to endure it. It's tough for me to reflect back on the countless and unfathomable things he did to me that I allowed. Most of them so cruel, I'm not even willing to detail a single one of them.

Regardless of how inconvenient it might be for me, Gene's needs, wants, and desires always came first. Many times, I would find myself questioning my saneness as he would turn on me and become completely apathetic with little or no notice or reason.

He would lie to me without any concern for the truth. Deceit was a frequent visitor to our relationship, and it showed up in the form of infidelities. I know of five. Lord only knows how many for sure.

He was most comfortable and masterful when talking about himself, irrespective of the achievements of others. He expected me to forgive and forget any behaviors he didn't want to admit to or be reminded of, especially in public settings. These are a few of the vast number of character flaws that I witnessed and faced during my association with Gene.

Every step of the way, I fought hard against my gut and allowed his atrocious conduct to continue. I had turned my back on my true self. I had walked away from my goodness and worthiness. I had become pathetic in my being. I forfeited twelve years—during the prime of my life—and, for ten of those years, I was living a lie.

You might ask, what the fuck was I thinking? It's a brilliant question, which I didn't entirely know the answer to at the time. Then the universe threw me a lifeline. George died.

PAUSE AND REFLECT: DON'T DO WHAT I DID

I implore you to have enough self-respect to not enter into or stay in a romantic relationship that is not wholesome and healthy. The most sensible and straightforward approach to having a thriving connection with a spouse or life partner is to have one with yourself first.

Consent to a journey into the vast spaces of your becoming. If you desire to be loved extravagantly by another, you must first love yourself to the same degree. Here is where I went wrong: I was accustomed to not feeling worthy enough to be loved elaborately. It is what I knew. Unfortunately, I failed to make this distinction until my dad died.

I knew something was amiss, but I was incapable of pinpointing what the source of my torment was. George's death was a threshold moment for me. I could remain myself, destitute of genuineness, or I could let the real me who was demanding emergence out of the cage that I had recklessly locked it into years earlier.

As you know, hindsight is 20/20. All of this relationship fiasco would have been averted if I had done some work on myself first. "Like what?" you might ask. Well, here is my short list:

Understanding and committing to self-love: I now know, and hopefully you do too, that it is impossible to have a nourishing relationship with anyone until you first have one with yourself. Without healthy regard for our well-being, we can easily fall prey to self-imposed dysfunctions or the bad behaviors of others.

It can take years to master self-love. You may have to unpack piles of limiting ideas that were likely formulated as a result of how you were raised and from past experiences. You have to be willing to confront any darkness within you and transform it into self-respect. Loving yourself is serious business; it is an ever-evolving process, and it is solely your responsibility. Remember, no one else is ever the cause of your problems.

A broad inquiry into my beliefs: This would have teased out my thoughts of deeming myself undeserving of deep and abiding love. Ugh, if I would have taken the time to dive into my feelings of unworthiness when they first started to appear, I could have saved myself from truckloads of heartache.

The trouble is, I was pretty damn young when I began to consider that all that I was, and all that I did, was not good enough. I didn't have access to the wisdom to know better. And, when I came of an age where I might discern that my thinking was bullshit, I had inadvertently allowed my thoughts of being unfit to be loved an influential role in my life.

This is a deep hole to crawl out of, so I encourage you not to go there in the first place. Now I know that how George and Gene treated me had nothing to do with me and everything to do with them. They were afraid, they lacked self-esteem, they were insecure, and they didn't know of or weren't willing to face their demons. I also know that each of us is on our own journey. I can give them space to be who they are, but I sure as hell do not have to share that space with them.

Clear identification and declaration of my values: What are your top three values? This is a question I have asked hundreds of times to potential candidates interested in being part of the team in my companies. Without exaggeration, ninety-nine percent of the people who have sat less than ten feet from me, when I inquire about their values, are stumped.

It is as if I am speaking a foreign language, one that they do not understand. Their answers vary. Some say, "I have no idea." Others say, "Wow, I have never been asked that before." Then, there are those who start pontificating because the silence in the room gets too uncomfortable for them to stomach.

Irrespective of their answer, I guarantee that they leave the interview and ponder this simple, yet rarely contemplated query. I like to think that their lives changed a little for the better because of our time together. For me, values are what is most important to me in my life.

Had I spent the time to name the primary things that are most important to me in life, I might have entered into my relationship with Gene, but I would not have remained there very long. I was one of those people who had no idea what my values were because I had never asked myself the question.

Today, I most certainly know what my answer to the question is. My values serve as an astute board of advisors who hold my feet to the fire when it comes to making choices and decisions. Do yourself a favor: ask, and answer, the question. Stick with it until you know for sure what is most important to you in your life and why.

There is a lot that we can do to ready ourselves to be in a relationship. Essential to a wholesome connection is being a whole person. The movies like to use one-liners like "you complete me" or "I want to be the reason behind your smile because surely you are the reason behind mine" or "you make me the happiest person in the world"—all of which bring to life one's deepest emotions or affections.

Scripts like this make for good ticket sales and put hope in the hearts of many who are desperately seeking fulfillment from someone outside of themselves. But everlasting love is not reliant on someone else, nor ought it be. Complete yourself, *be* the reason behind "your" smile, allow yourself to *be* the happiest person in the world. It is when you have accomplished these things that you are ready to consider teaming up with another.

Chapter Twenty-Nine

My Lightbulb Moment

"She was finally ok, or at least she believed. She had no idea where she was going, but she sure knows where she's been and anywhere was better than that."

— JmStorm

GENE ATTENDED GEORGE'S funeral with me. I remember sitting next to him at the cemetery, looking over at one point during the burial service to see he was sobbing. I found this to be odd, especially given he had never met George. He had never even had a conversation with him. Plus, he knew my history with my dad.

The day ended at my mom's house. While my brothers, mom, and sister-in-law and I sat up and chatted about the day—the services, and our memories of George—Gene went to bed. He couldn't stand the fact that the conversation didn't revolve around him.

The next day we went for a walk, and I asked him why he was so upset at the services. He explained to me that, even though he didn't know George, his death reminded him of his mortality. And there it was. Gene was mourning his own impermanence.

He was so self-centered that, regardless of the circumstances of the situation, he had to make it about himself. What a fucked-up way to live. A few days after we returned home from the funeral, I took my dogs for a walk, pondering the previous few days. Then, BAM! I had an epiphany. It came to me in an instant.

I realized, now that George was gone, I was never going to be treated poorly by a man—or anyone, for that matter—ever again. I had somehow plugged into the idea that as long as George was alive, I didn't deserve to be admired and cherished by a man.

I know that may sound like an exceedingly preposterous notion, but it was the world I chose for myself for the previous twelve years of my life. In hindsight, it made sense to me. I had ultimately decided to be with a man who was just like George. Ugh. Sometimes life can be a shit sandwich, and I had made a full-on banquet out of it. Twice.

This insight changed me at the very moment it had come to me. I turned on my heels and hastily walked back home. My stride was light, yet confident. A newfound conviction came over me; I could feel it in every cell of my body. When I got to the house, I located Gene sitting in one of the bedrooms watching TV.

I walked into the room and said, "Guess what? I just figured something out. While I was out walking, a flash of clarity and understanding came to me. It occurred to me now that George is dead, I won't allow anyone to mistreat me again, especially a man."

For the first time in twelve years, I had reclaimed my power, and Gene knew it. His demeanor shifted. He didn't say anything. He didn't have to, as his eyes gave away everything he was thinking. My words shocked him. He knew the proverbial "Annie-will-put-up-with-my-shit" party was over.

It was on this day our relationship started to unravel. For the next several months, we managed to move through our days as a couple, trying to make things work. But it's hard for a master manipulator to concede their shortcomings, particularly when they view themselves as having been knocked off their pedestal.

Gene and I stuck it out through the fire and the loss of my house, but it was as if we were both slogging through thick, heavy mud. As I was going through the process of designing and rebuilding my house, I endeavored to include Gene in the details and decision-making as much as possible. His participation and enthusiasm waned as the months went by.

To his credit, he was also rebuilding a small rental property he owned, destroyed by the same fire. The challenge came when I was making choices about the new house, overseeing the construction, and managing the building budget. You see, it was my house—not our house, and certainly not Gene's house.

However, as you might expect by now, he did his best to make it appear to the outside world that it was his house and that he was the genius behind what turned out to be a spectacular home for me. The truth is, Gene wasn't nearly the phenomenon he thought he was. The few things I let Gene take charge of all turned out to be a fiasco in the long run.

The guy who thought he was the smartest person in the room, who was spending my money, turned in a lackluster performance every time, without fail. We took one final run at preserving our relationship before its ultimate ruin. Friends of mine had recommended a psychologist who specialized in couple's therapy.

Gene and I were not living together at the time and hadn't been for several months. We were three sessions in on our counseling attempt, which was going okay, but not spectacular. The therapist had given both of us homework to do, which I liked and was always eager to complete.

I met Gene at the therapist's office for session number four. I could tell right away something was wrong; he was dismissive and curt when I greeted him. After we walked into the room and got settled, the therapist asked a question to start our meeting.

Gene rudely interrupted her and said that he would not be staying, but he wanted to read something to us before he left. I don't remember the particulars of his self-serving lecture, but that is exactly what it was: a lecture. He delivered it with the same bravado and accusation as a defense attorney bidding to convince a jury their client is innocent when, in fact, they're guilty as hell.

The irony of Gene's performance was that he was guilty as hell. His homework assignment was to disclose and expound on his perfidies. Gene's flare-up was typical of his need to construct a defensive facade to protect his rickety self-esteem. This assignment made him feel inferior.

He was not capable of admitting to his mistakes and apologizing for them, so, in turn, he became grandiose. He needed to insist on his omnipotence, devaluing our therapist, and (of course) me.

Satisfied with his holier-than-thou sermon, Gene rode out of the therapist's office on his high horse, never to return. I stayed. I'd been on the receiving end of Gene's acts of arrogant superiority many times. The therapist asked me how I felt about the incident. I told her I was not at all surprised by his conduct and predicted he was already on his cell phone talking to another woman, who would most likely be in his bed that night.

I told her I felt I had done my best to keep this poorly chosen connection with Gene going. I said that I knew in my gut that it was time to move on. And I had known it for a very long time. I expressed my desire to redesign my life and put an end to the existence that was currently me.

I articulated to her my need to stop showing up in my life as pitiful and that instead, it was time to step up to the plate and get real. *It was time for me to go home to myself.* I knew that it wasn't going to be seashells and balloons as I began this long-overdue journey back to who I was, but I was ready, despite the bloodiness and brokenness and sheer terror that I would face along the way.

Recapturing my authenticity was a battle I was willing to fight because I knew my life depended on it. When I finished talking, she sat across the room from me with tears in her eyes, nodding her head in agreement, and assured me that I was a warrior and that this was a war I would win.

We stood up together as our session came to an end and embraced each other. She told me to stay in touch, but there was no need to return. We both knew I would bump into unpredictable peril on my deployment into the harsh landscape of renewed self-discovery, but I was ready for it.

Although I knew, without question, my relationship with Gene must end, I still went through many months of feeling despair. To some degree, the anguish came from being addicted to unworthiness. I slowly acknowledged and accepted the emptiness inside me, making room for truth and freedom.

In this space, God's voice became distinct and offered me the peace and certainty I was seeking. I realized that the hollowness, as unpleasant as it was, would one day become fertile ground for my deserted authenticity to take root once again and flourish.

My inner chaos gradually gave way to fully embracing heartbreak. Heartbreak evolved into vulnerability, and vulnerability advanced my trust in my voyage back to my truth. There is a great line written by the poet Anaïs Nin that says: "*And the day came when the risk to remain tight in a bud was more painful than the risk it took to blossom.*"

I experienced this firsthand. It was too painful for me to continue to be the person I was being. So, I chose to allow the unfolding of my becoming whole and worthy. Eventually, I came to know that you will always be too much for anyone not enough.

PAUSE AND REFLECT: THE ART OF UN-BECOMING

"The path of awakening is not about becoming who you are. Rather, it is about unbecoming who you are not."
— Albert Schweitzer

Most of us are so attached to who we are that we never see the potential of who we can be. As I was traversing through the rugged terrain of coming home to myself, one of the things I did was to question all that I had come to believe in my life.

I wanted to make sure I wasn't just going through the motions of my days on earth. I wanted to start fresh and unwind any philosophies I had created that were not serving me. I started to examine my viewpoints in nine domains of my life.

1. I asked myself what family represented in my life and how I wanted to show up for my loved ones moving forward.
2. I evaluated my friendships and associations, and I committed to letting go of those that were toxic or lacked integrity on any level, and I would nourish those based on mutual respect and support.
3. I promised myself that, should I choose to enter into a romantic relationship with a man, it would be only if the connection turned up the volume on my already-fantastic life.
4. I would hold my feet to the fire and never succumb to outside pressures when it came to my chosen vocations. I was not interested in a job or a career, and I would never identify my service in the world as work.
5. I was determined not to be a slave to money. Instead, I would allow great abundance to flow to me as a result of the contribution I was making.
6. I would honor my physical health and practice wholesome habits that would ensure a life of vigor and wellness.
7. I would be an apprentice of the heroes and heroines that came before me who have left behind nuggets of a well-lived and complete life as I pursued my avenues of personal development.
8. I would force myself out of my comfort zone to embark on creativity and learning opportunities I previously hadn't considered.

9. And finally, I would allow myself more recreation and leisure time (this one was the most confronting to me).

These pledges were my promises to eliminate the gap between my inner North Star and my outer behavior. I needed to do these things to cultivate a strategy of authenticity that was the real deal. This was "keep your ass in the saddle" stuff. It was all part of un-becoming, paring down, and getting rid of emotional clutter that kept my soul in the basement hidden from all that mattered.

As I went through the process of redesigning my life, I noticed a lightness of my being. The tightness in my chest gave way to an openness to love myself with the same extravagance as God did. The storm of my fears and uncertainties had come to an end, and a great calm came over me. There was a thankfulness. I had come to contentment in myself, and I was happy.

It is my sincere hope that you will come to this same place in your life. I am confident that you will discover the same relief and liberty in your living that I have come to know in my life. I am your biggest fan, regardless of where you are on your path of un-becoming.

Chapter Thirty

CHANGE

"Change is neither good or bad. It simply is."

— Don Draper

ABOUT THE KIDS

IT IS MY humble observation that the lessons I learned from my up-bringing on the farm are missing in today's fast-paced, technology-ridden, modern world. Kids today lack guidance and discipline from their parents. And I can see why. Many parents lack direction and self-control in their own lives.

So many people have grown accustomed to immediate gratification, and they approach life with an "I want it now" attitude. We have information, food, movies, and just about anything we can shop for online at our fingertips and at our front door within minutes or hours of pushing a button on our smartphones. We have an expectation of fast results with no need or desire to earn it.

I understand that culture and mindsets change over time. It's an inevitable by-product of evolution and advancements in the way we live our lives. However, what I don't think needs to change are the key and foundational constructs of living a fulfilling and authentic life.

Ignoring or never being taught these fundamentals in the first place is where I believe we have gone off the rails into what seems to be a messy and self-serving approach to our existence.

I consider the feminist movement of the 1960s and 1970s to be the start of a transition in our country that was necessary and positive. And, as with most matters of far-reaching change, anything taken to an extreme can give rise to unintended consequences.

I support the majority of the reforms accomplished by this crusade, and those who have led the charge. The fact that women decided they wanted to use their skills and knowledge to make valuable contributions to society, as well as to pursue fulfilling vocations, gets a thumbs-up from me.

However, this turning point, as progressive and seemingly positive as it appeared to be, brought with it deviations from the traditional family structure. And, in many ways, ushered in a new and troubling child-rearing model. Women could now "have it all."

They could be a wife, a mother, and have a satisfying career. In theory, it appeared to be an admirable existence. However, in reality, it's been my observation that you can have it all, just not all at once. Women entering the workforce left babies and young children in the hands of babysitters or daycare facilities.

As well-meaning and dedicated as those folks are, it is not the same as the focused attention of a mother or father. When these kids were old enough to be in school for the bulk of the day, they came home to an empty house and became identified as "latchkey" kids.

Moms and dads would come home, tired from their day at work, consequently putting in little time or energy to be attentive to the children. When children are ages zero through five, they are the most impressionable. They rely heavily on whoever is raising them for guidance and discipline.

In large part, these five years are the foundation upon which the rest of a child's life evolves. It is during these years that children pay close attention to what parents and others say and how they act. They are human sponges that take it all in, but they don't have the emotional tools and maturity to filter through the vast amount of bullshit thrown at them by their hopefully well-intended parents and the outside world.

Whatever happened to allowing children to be authentic? Instead of forcing them to do and be what we want them to do and be, how about just letting them "be," and supporting the process of their natural strengths coming to the surface? Whatever happened to teaching them resilience by allowing them to fall and fail?

How about explaining to them that when they come in second, they don't get a trophy? What about permitting them to suffer the consequences of their bad choices instead of swooping in and fixing everything for them? How about teaching them to earn the things they want instead of just buying them whatever they want, whenever they want it?

How about playing and talking and connecting with them through steadfast presence? How about saying "fuck you" to society's measures of success and help your children determine what their values are? THEIRS. Not yours, not the neighbor's, not other parents', not some intangible source or some so-called expert. How about teaching them not to compare themselves to others?

That is a waste of time. Instead, teach them to compare themselves to their best self and encourage them to embrace their worthiness. Guide them, so that one day they can confidently guide themselves. You are your child's most important teacher. Not some private coach or tutor: YOU.

About YOU

Does this sound like work to you? Well, it is. And therein lies the challenge. Are you willing to put the effort in as a parent? If so, you are going to have to put your cell phone down, turn off the TV, and unplug from any external commotion. You are going to need to be entirely focused and attentive.

You are going to have to stop comparing yourself to others. You are going to have to be brutally honest with yourself. And, you are going to need to get comfortable with being uncomfortable. In writing these words, I am addressing all of us, including myself, not just "parents."

To create a life that you love, you must start being accountable for the choices you make because every single one of those choices has contributed to what your life looks and feels like today. You must become your own hero. YOU are the only person who has the ability to change your life.

Yes, fear will raise its ugly head. Know that and be brave anyway. Temptation will knock at the door. Know that and say, "No." Decide that you are no longer going to play small. Pick yourself up and dust yourself off. Your past does not have to dictate your future. Let that shit go.

Talk to yourself like you love yourself, and mean it. Show up for yourself each day. Start now. Not tomorrow, not in ten minutes—now. You owe it to yourself to make your days count. If ever there was a time to dare to be all that you can be, it is now.

Embark on this journey; you are worthy. There will be good days and bad days and sad days and glad days. Most things worth doing come with a few challenges along the way. Do not give up. Be your own hero, because YOU are worth fighting for.

Chapter Thirty-One

———∽∽∼———

COMING FULL CIRCLE

"We've come full circle, but the conditions have changed."
— Bob Peterson

AFTER LEARNING OF George's death, I told Dan I would get right to work booking a flight. The next morning, I boarded a plane headed to Denver to bury the man who brought me into this world. During the two-and-a-half-hour flight, I remember sitting in my seat thinking how odd it was to be so emotionless about the death of this guy known as my dad.

Dan and my sister-in-law picked me up at the airport, and we headed straight to George's attorney's office. Dan and I took our seats across the table from a gentleman who appeared to be practical and professional as he read George's last will and testament to us.

We sat there as the words "you have been intentionally disinherited" pierced through the otherwise silent room. In his last hurtful move, George made it clear he was disowning Dan and me, leaving his entire estate to Mike. Neither of us flinched. We nodded as the attorney paused to ask us how we felt about our disinheritance.

What were we supposed to say? Or do? Pop open a bottle of champagne and celebrate? We both concurred we would honor and respect George's wishes, so if that was it, we were taking off. After all, we had a funeral to plan.

You never know what's in the heart and mind of another. I've come to know that what other people think or say about us has nothing to do with us, but everything to do with them. Why would George divest two of his children? I don't know, and I haven't spent a whole lot of time thinking about it. I never expected I deserved or should get anything as the result of my dad dying.

When I left home at seventeen, I figured I needed to find a way to provide for myself; it was no longer my parents' job. From that point forward, my life was on me. So, hearing those words in the attorney's office that day was not astounding to me. I guess you could say my relationship with George was not the typical father-daughter relationship.

And—oddly—that's been a good thing for me for a whole lot of reasons. This man—in his selfish, distant ways—made me the strong woman I am today. I remember walking from my house to my barn a few years ago. It was a Sunday, and it was Father's Day.

For reasons unbeknownst to me, and for the first time in decades, I thought about this day, set aside to honor fathers and celebrate fatherhood. I paused for a few minutes to thank George. After all, without him, there would be no me. I thanked him for all he taught me as a young girl on the farm.

I thanked him for being an example of how I didn't want to be in my own life. I thanked him for being who he was because it helped me to evolve into who I am. I thanked him for Dan, the best brother a girl could ever have. I thanked him for being a heavy-handed dad because it taught me to be a whole-hearted woman.

I thanked him for disowning me because it allowed me full ownership of my being. And—finally—I thanked him for dying because that's when I decided to start living. On this particular Father's Day, I set us both free. Free from guilt, blame, and misunderstanding; needing to be right, discomfort, and unknowing. When I got back to the house, I popped open a bottle of wine and celebrated. It wasn't champagne, but it was close enough.

You see, at some point shortly after our eighteenth birthday, I think we have to take charge of our own life. We have to stop blaming others for our lot in life. We have to step up and look bravely into discomfort, vulnerability, and truth. Instead of pointing our fingers out into the world and accusing external factors for any dissatisfaction in our lives, we have to stand in front of a mirror and ask:

- *What are you going to do to create a life that you love?*
- *What are you going to do that will contribute to your happiness?*
- *What are you going to do to be accountable for your life?*
- *What are you going to do to make the world a better place?*

The answers to these questions create our truth, which in turn opens up the flood gates to our genuineness. I believe the secret to authenticity is tearing down the barriers amid our inner feelings and our external expression of ourselves.

So often we endure life by posing as a forged self instead of our true essence. We present a false identity for the rest of the world to see. At some point, we have to resolve to be our real self. Otherwise, we'll live in a self-constructed prison. When we allow courage to come alive, the walls we previously built around us crumble and transform into frontiers of possibility.

I am not sure how this book found its way into your hands. I am simply thankful that it did. It is my hope that somewhere among these pages you found solace, or encouragement, or desire, or inspiration, or the willingness to become your best self. Ultimately, life is about choices.

At any given moment you have the capability to reinvent your destiny. Your destiny reveals itself according to the choices you make. It is my wish that you dare to look inside yourself. That is where the awakening starts. Take responsibility for each of your thoughts. As you do this, you will mindfully remove all of your inner turbulence.

Explore your talents and apply your God-given gifts in ways that serve others. Reclaim your joy and zest for living. Be yourself. There is zero nobility in seeking to be like someone else. True nobility comes from your relentless and unwavering intention and inspired actions to be better than you were yesterday.

Don't wait. Start your journey today. Step into your mastery. Know that the potential for extraordinary abundance and achievement and lasting fulfillment lies within you. And, last but not least: keep your ass in the saddle.

Chapter Thirty-Two

———— ✺ ————

AFTER THE STORM

IN HIS BOOK *Kafka on the Shore*, Haruki Murakami wrote the following:

Sometimes fate is like a small sandstorm that keeps changing directions. You change direction but the sandstorm chases you. You turn again, but the storm adjusts. Over and over you play this out, like some ominous dance with death just before dawn. Why? Because this storm isn't something that blew in from far away, something that has nothing to do with you. This storm is you. Something inside of you. So all you can do is give in to it, step right inside the storm, closing your eyes and plugging up your ears so the sand doesn't get in, and walk through it, step by step. There's no sun there, no moon, no direction, no sense of time. Just fine white sand swirling up into the sky like pulverized bones. That's the kind of sandstorm you need to imagine.

And you really will have to make it through that violent, metaphysical, symbolic storm. No matter how metaphysical or symbolic it might be, make no mistake about it: it will cut through flesh like a thousand razor blades. People will bleed there, and you will bleed too. Hot, red blood. You'll catch that blood in your hands, your own blood and the blood of others.

And once the storm is over you won't remember how you made it through, how you managed to survive. You won't even be sure, in fact, whether the storm is really over. But one thing is certain. When you come out of the storm you won't be the same person who walked in. That's what this storm's all about.

All that I have depicted on the previous pages describes my metaphorical sandstorm. It took me a couple of handfuls of uneasy months to remember where I was and what I was doing here. Not long after I had established and committed to my "Lines in the Sand," I was riding horses with a friend of mine. I was telling her about these lines and my dedication to living my life according to them, and she said that I needed to share them with people. She felt that my story and my journey would be inspiring and valuable to others. I told her that I created these guideposts to save myself and that I had no intention of sharing them with others. And, I wasn't looking for something else to do.

But as I thought about it more, I decided why not? Why not help others if I could? So, I got industrious and developed the curriculum and the content for a year-long live class. I gathered 10 of my gal pals and asked if they would commit to one day a month for a year to come to my barn and participate in the class. During that year, I witnessed a beautiful transformation in these women.

They became freer, happier, softer, forgiving, and brave people. They let go of things that didn't matter and enhanced the things that did. They started to choose love over fear, and most importantly, they became gentler with themselves and found their true essence.

We live in a fast-paced, chaotic world with information about anything at our fingertips 24/7. I don't think humans are built to handle the speed, chaos, distraction, and noise of the world. We don't develop the resources we need to manage the overwhelm. Most people are so busy building empires that they don't take time to build self-esteem.

They are focused on having the "next best thing" *instead of becoming their next best self.* They want bigger and better stuff instead of a bigger and better heart. My aim with the "Lines" is to bestow upon myself and others a values-based framework—guidelines that will assist us in keeping our ass in the saddle.

Since those 10 women sat in my barn with me, I have continued to offer the live class, and it is one of my favorite ways to spend my time. After teaching it a handful of times, the participates urged me to design an online version of the course so that people all over the world would have access to it.

Once again, I had not envisioned crafting an online program. Remember? I only wanted to save myself. Yet the notion seemed like the natural progression of this excursion on which I found myself. So, with absolutely no idea about what I was doing or how to do it, I put one foot in front of the other, day after day.

Who said God is rational as he presents us with opportunities of self-discovery beyond our wildest imagination? By now I should have been used to Divinity colliding with my self-appointed life plans. Who knows why we say yes? As the dust continued to settle from my storm, I began to realize that I had morphed into mindfully serving others.

So, with the help of a talented web designer, we launched Meet Me At The Barn, a web-based self-mastery and personal development program intended to help people of purpose achieve their highest level of living. The website offers the Lines in the Sand course, a 21-Day Authenticity Challenge, the Badass Soul Seeking Warrior podcast, and other content and resources to assist people in creating a life that they love.

Being uncomfortable is breathtaking. It feels wobbly. It holds certainty hostage from any promise of relief. And yet, the greatest blessings in my life have shown up on the other side of my uneasy passages through distress. It is no different than a seed that is placed in the soil with dirt thrown over it.

There is some struggle involved in sprouting from the darkness to reach the light. The butterfly experiences some unpleasantness as it grapples with its transformation from a cocoon to a state of beauty and freedom. I have reminded myself of this many times since embarking on the redesign of my life.

Yes, there were many awkward times as I decided to share my story with others. Putting my personal "Lines in the Sand" into a format that could be revealed to others in a manner that was embraceable and valuable to them was something I had never done before. Being the vessel from which what I had learned on my own trek back to authenticity so it could be shared with people was a first for me.

Balancing vulnerability with trust as I guide participants to choose to live their best life puts me back to square one each time I teach. Transforming the live class experience into a digital construct that was supportive and sensible came with no prior knowledge of how to do such a thing. My not knowing how to do any of this was interwoven with as much uncertainty as a willingness to move forward and believe that my desire to help others would somehow fall into place.

I tell you this because I want you to hang in there when you have an aspiration that means so much to you, and at the same time, it feels daunting. You are capable of doing anything that you wish. And guess what? Along the way, you will run into naysayers. There will be people who will tell you that you are crazy or that your idea will never work.

March on regardless. Don't plug into the negativity of others. Instead, listen to your voice and trust your gut. Yes, there will be discouraging days; it is part of the process. Don't let it stop you from stepping fully into the vision you have for your life. Never question your authenticity or apologize for your ambition.

In addition to having created Meet Me At The Barn, my business partner, Kate, and I continue to own and operate our physical therapy and wellness facility in the San Diego area. I am very proud of this company. What we do is unique. Our model for delivering patient care and education is deeply rooted in core values of integrity, passion, professionalism, trust, and fun. We are fortunate to have hand-selected a dedicated team of people who show up each day devoted to helping others achieve their highest level of health and wellness. We desire that the legacy of what we have fashioned carries on far beyond our involvement. Each conversation, meeting, and other inspired action happens with this in mind.

The farmer in me is alive and well. Not a day goes by that I don't pinch myself noting the pure gratefulness I have for being the steward of my little slice of land in Southern California. Many years ago after I purchased this property, I named it Painted Sky Ranch. The reasoning is twofold. One, I am the proud owner and custodian of two retired ranch horses, Chief and Winston.

They both captured my heart the moment that I saw them, and they have been such loyal and wise teachers over the years. Chief is a beautiful "paint" horse with a regal stature and stunning markings who adds rich character to the ranch. Two, most evenings I have a front-row seat to the most glorious sunsets imaginable. As the day hands off the baton to the moon and the stars, the sky is painted with colors for which only God can be given credit. Hence, Painted Sky Ranch.

I believe that this sacred place selected me as much as I picked it. Out of choice, I am the primary caretaker of my property. It's a lot. There is always something to do whether it is mowing the riverbed, pulling weeds, mending a fence, or changing the oil in my tractor.

Many folks have asked me why I don't "have other people do the work?" Well, for me, it is out of honor and appreciation that at least for now, this land is mine. It is an expression of who I am and an echo of my past—a wholesome Midwestern upbringing. The work is not a duty, but a privilege that I will selfishly grasp on to for as long as I can.

Assigning these tasks to others would be an abandonment of all that nurtures my soul. Standing on real dirt, and digging in it, and smelling it is grounding and reassuring, and simple, and necessary for me. So, for as long as my bones and body agree, I will continue my dance with the land.

My relationship status continues to be "single." I am happy and content with this being the case. I find that there is tremendous liberty and solitude in my life without partnership. I am not opposed to the possibility of a relationship, but it is not something that I am in search of or that I long for. Why? you might ask. Because in the process of redesigning my life, I developed a deep understanding and appreciation for what matters most to me. Being at peace and living with joy has become paramount to my existence.

Every decision I make is based on maintaining this level of living. I do not depend on "someone" to make me happy. My happiness is my responsibility. Not someone else's. Over the years, I have been witness to far too many men and women thinking that they couldn't be happy until they found the right partner or husband or wife.

They entered into relationships as unfulfilled people and guess what? They remained unfulfilled, which led to the untethering of the very relationship that they swore was the answer to their happiness.

Here's the deal. Get to know yourself. Fall in love with yourself. Learn to appreciate and respect yourself. Take care of and nurture yourself. Enjoy yourself. And, most importantly, be yourself. And then, when someone comes along who acknowledges and appreciates who you are and turns the volume up on your already fulfilling life, you may want to consider getting to know them better.

I am surrounded by beautiful examples of happy and thriving relationships and marriages. I have great respect and adoration for men. And I am a big fan of love. Is it in the cards for me? I don't know. Time will tell. I have an unshakeable trust in "what is meant to be will be." And, I am going to continue to enjoy the shit out of life.

Haruki Murakami is right:

I am not the same person who walked into my storm. As disruptive and confusing and painful as the storm was, I came out the other side a more evolved person. There is not a day that goes by that I don't thank God for all the beauty and blessings that my storm brought to me. Now each day I stand naked with grace and allow my humanness the time and space that it needs for growth and understanding. Please do the same for yourself.

Stanley Kunitz wrote this beautiful poem called "The Layers." Here it is:

I have walked through many lives,
some of them my own,
and I am not who I was,
though some principle of being
abides, from which I struggle
not to stray.
When I look behind,
as I am compelled to look
before I can gather strength
to proceed on my journey,
I see the milestones dwindling
toward the horizon
and the slow fires trailing
from the abandoned camp-sites,
over which scavenger angels
wheel on heavy wings.
Oh, I have made myself a tribe
out of my true affections,
and my tribe is scattered!
How shall the heart be reconciled
to its feast of losses?
In a rising wind
the manic dust of my friends,
those who fell along the way,
bitterly stings my face.
Yet I turn, I turn,
exulting somewhat,

with my will intact to go
wherever I need to go,
and every stone on the road
precious to me.
In my darkest night,
when the moon was covered
and I roamed through wreckage,
a nimbus-clouded voice
directed me:
"Live in the layers,
not on the litter."
Though I lack the art
to decipher it,
no doubt the next chapter
in my book of transformations
is already written.
I am not done with my changes.

This, I know for sure: I am not done with my changes, either.

You're Invited

Please visit:

www.meetmeatthebarn.com/tools

Here you will find wholehearted and wholesome tools, resources, and coaching that will assist you in creating a life that you love.

Please join:

www.meetmeatthebarn.com/community

The online community is a place where like-minded people gather for a compassionate exchange of ideas as well as inspiration and encouragement to live life up to our full potential.

CPSIA information can be obtained
at www.ICGtesting.com
Printed in the USA
FSHW011256200721
83387FS

9 781977 215246